On a Kenya Ranch

Ian Guy Patrick Grant

On a Kenya Ranch

LAVINIA GRANT

Towseler   Tess

Murray, Kaberia, Bisharo and others playing in back yard

PIONEER ASSOCIATES

to Guy

Published in Great Britain in 2001 by
Pioneer Associates (Graphic) Limited
Old Sawmill
Camserney By Aberfeldy
Perthshire
PH15 2JF

Copyright © Lavinia Grant 2001

All rights reserved. No part of this book may be reproduced or transmitted in any form or by any means, electronic or mechanical, including photocopying, recording, or by any information storage and retrieval system, without permission in writing from the publisher.

British Library Cataloguing-in-Publication Data

A catalogue record for this book is available from the British Library

ISBN 0-9540085-0-2

Designed and typeset by Pioneer Associates, Perthshire and printed and bound in Singapore under the supervision of MRM Graphics, Winslow, Buckinghamshire

Published in conjunction with Elizabeth Blair

By the same author, 'Nyamuluki, a small piece of Africa'

Contents

Author's Note	vii
Some History and The Land	1
The Men and Livestock	13
Our Home	34
The Town	44
The Children	50
Walking in The Bush	60
Animal Stories (*Dogs – Horses – Cats*)	67
'Kilo-Foxtrot November'	85
Some Birds (*Icarus – Poultry – Platypus*)	89
Fire, Drought, Rain and River	100
Chirpie	111
Past, Future, and a White Rainbow	116

A MAP OF EL KARAMA RANCH
(not to scale)
14.152 acres

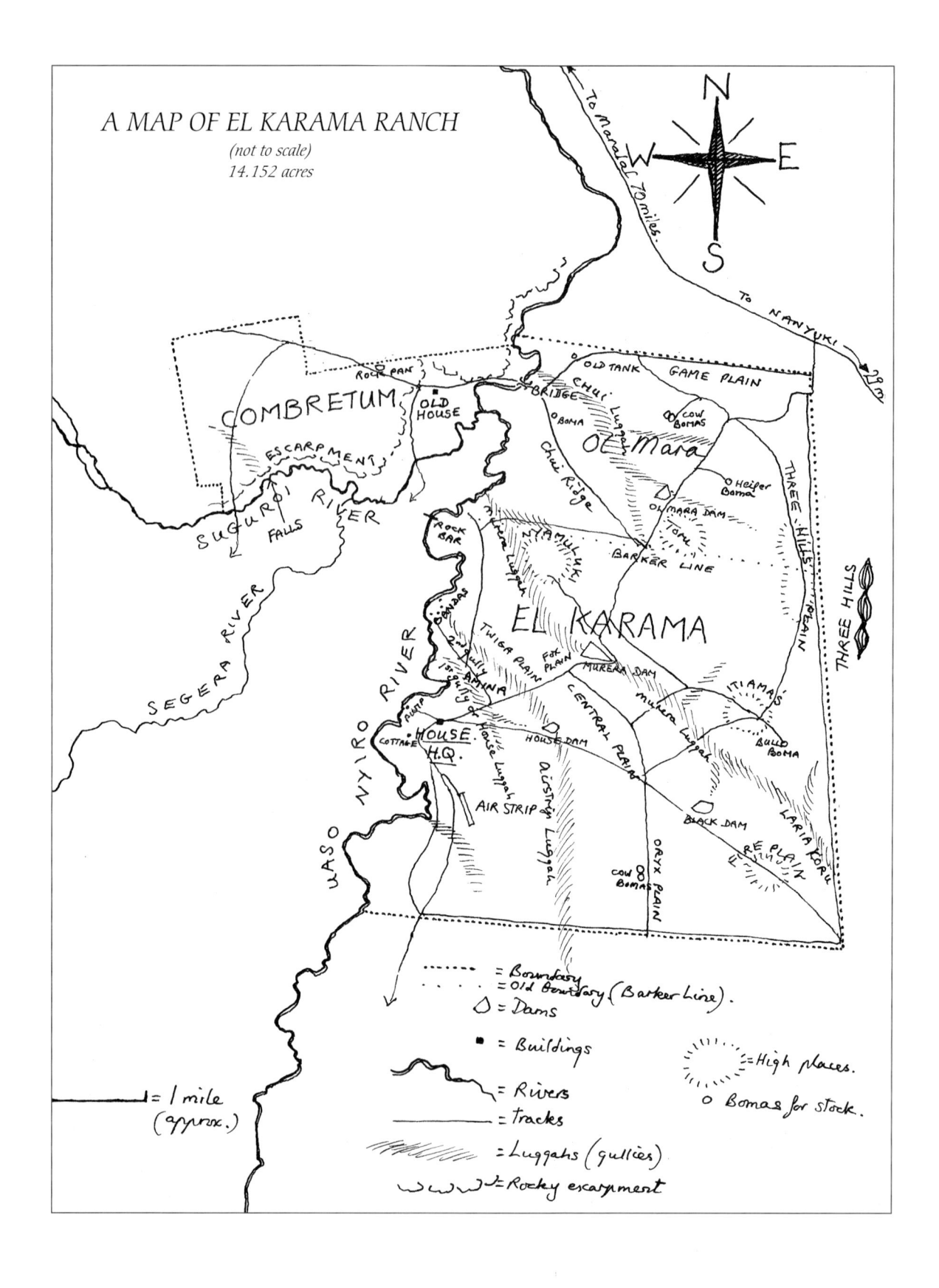

Author's Note

El Karama, a ranch in Kenya, was described previously as 'Nyamuluki' in *A Small Piece of Africa*. But here, I tell more of our home, something of our lives and of those who work here, of our animals, and a little of ranching itself in that same natural setting. It is a lighthearted patchwork, of a personal rather than historic nature, written mainly for the family. But from the questions that are often asked, I felt encouraged that others might be interested, too. And I had the desire to try to express in words, drawings and paintings something more of the rainbow quality of this place where we are lucky enough to live, and to record some of its ways in case, one day, they are lost.

❋

It was March 1969. The jet from Bombay was lumbering towards Nairobi above, and sometimes in, a counterpane of cloud. The nearer clouds seemed to move fast like veils whisked away, and under them was a slower-moving, softer denseness. As the big aeroplane felt its way carefully downwards, with my face pressed to the window I saw through a sudden dizzy hole in the clouds, far below to the ground. There was a greenish-khaki sea of grass and it seemed that heat was coming up from it, warming and vibrant. And in the very middle of this cloud-window was a Maasai encampment of cattle enclosures, the reddish mud-and-dung huts built into the circular brush walls. In that second I saw Africa with the whole of my being, and felt, with the romantic intensity of youth, that I was coming home – though why this should have been so I did not pause to wonder. It was all far too exciting.

I was visiting Kenya from India to see African wild life, and planned to meet a friend there who was a cousin of Guy Grant. We were to visit Guy, whom I had not met, during our stay, but the cousin was unable to come to Kenya after all. Nina and Hugh Mitchell, old family friends, invited me to stay with them in their mud-brick, colonial bungalow on their coffee and sisal plantation at Makuyu, near Thika. The house was full of interesting insects, and Nina would fearlessly catch the big flat spiders off my bedroom walls and remove them, before I could sleep. She reprimanded me, for allowing mosquitoes to bite so I could see how their mouth-parts worked, in case I got malaria. Hugh warned me that I would catch jiggers when I walked barefoot. The garden was full of wonderful birds that I had never seen before – Cinnamon-chested bee-eaters, Violet-crested turacos, White-headed barbets, Mouse birds and Striped swallows. The view from the house swept in a great curve over the dark coffee bushes and away, smoky-blue with distance, to the indigo roots of Mount Kenya towering into a mysterious haze of cloud which always hid the summit. I did not know then that soon I would live beyond that mountain.

From the Mitchells I went on safari through the Mara to the Serengeti, and back via Amboseli. After that it was time to go home to Scotland. But Nina, who knew Guy's family, persuaded me to visit him before leaving in spite of the non-appearance of his cousin. She had a feeling that Guy and I would get on well together, though she did not tell me then. Nina was right! We were married the next year and by September 1970 were on our way home to the ranch after our honeymoon.

Bush babies

Some History and The Land

It is called El Karama which, according to the old Swahili dictionary, is Arabic in origin and means 'Something of honour, an answer to prayer, a treasured possession'. It was named by Paddy Batelle, an Irish soldier settler, who drew his lot for this land out of a hat at the end of the First World War, and came here slowly, for there were no roads in Laikipia then, with his mules and oxen. He built the first small house from blocks of golden sandstone, which today is our sitting room. The bush lapped up to its very door, and over the door was fastened, as it still is, the shoe of a mule. Around the house was nothing but the whistling-thorns and the wild grasses, through which ran the sibilant wind; the cushions and stars of the wild flowers were its garden.

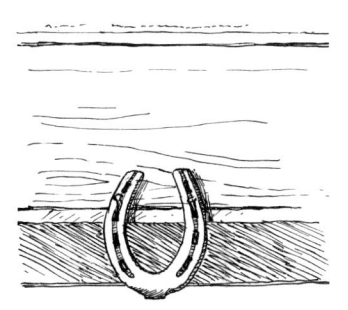

Mule's shoe over door

Ox Wagon

Although Paddy Batelle and his wife must have loved the place to call it El Karama, they did not stay long and during that time Mrs. Batelle, a charming woman we have heard, nearly died of malaria which was misdiagnosed as 'flu by the 'local' doctor, also recently arrived from Ireland. Perhaps the struggle to establish the ranch and make a living from the bush was too much for the Batelles. It would have been an arduous journey to Nairobi, then a growing railhead town, and the fledgling village of Nanyuki (normally an hour's bumpy drive away today, though sometimes much longer) would have taken at least two days to reach with oxen. So, around the year 1925, the Batelles returned to Ireland. There used to be a disintegrating trough in the back yard upon which was engraved the letters P.J.B. and the date – 1920. This initialled block now forms the doorstep to the saddle room by our garden gate.

The Osbornes came next to El Karama. Mrs. Osborne was of the Randall family who were amongst the first Europeans to settle the

Saddle-room door

Falkirk cauldrons, used in early days for cooking on open fires

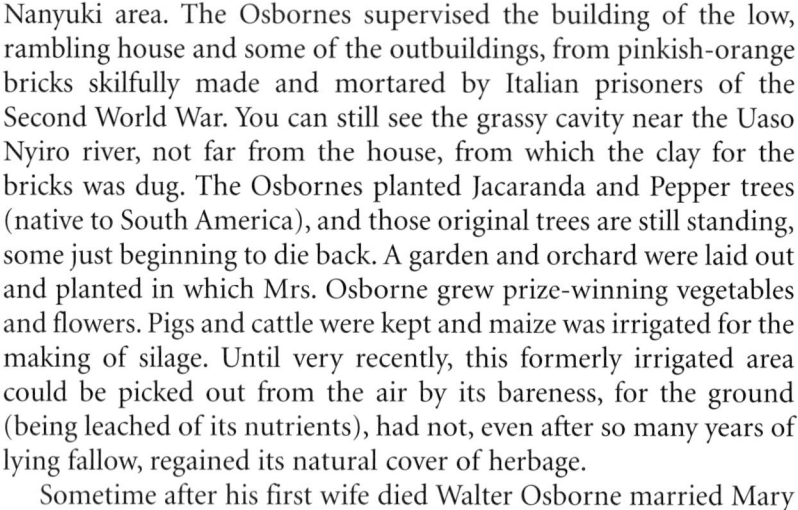

Yoke for oxen

Nanyuki area. The Osbornes supervised the building of the low, rambling house and some of the outbuildings, from pinkish-orange bricks skilfully made and mortared by Italian prisoners of the Second World War. You can still see the grassy cavity near the Uaso Nyiro river, not far from the house, from which the clay for the bricks was dug. The Osbornes planted Jacaranda and Pepper trees (native to South America), and those original trees are still standing, some just beginning to die back. A garden and orchard were laid out and planted in which Mrs. Osborne grew prize-winning vegetables and flowers. Pigs and cattle were kept and maize was irrigated for the making of silage. Until very recently, this formerly irrigated area could be picked out from the air by its bareness, for the ground (being leached of its nutrients), had not, even after so many years of lying fallow, regained its natural cover of herbage.

Sometime after his first wife died Walter Osborne married Mary Abrams, and they moved to South Africa with their new young family before Kenya gained independence in 1963, when the second son of the first marriage, Basil, on behalf of his father, sold El Karama to Guy Grant. Guy bought it with the help of Land Bank and agricultural Finance Corporation loans which took him twenty years of hard work to repay, and with the aid of partnerships.

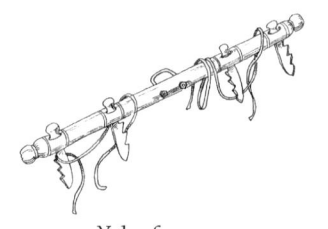

Guy was born in Nairobi in 1928. His father, Hugh Grant, had come to Kenya in 1922, seconded to the King's African Rifles after serving in Russia and with the Cameron Highlanders through the First World War. Soon he realised that peacetime soldiering was not for him. He retired from the army, but having fallen in love with Kenya he went into a tea planting partnership which failed to work out. During this venture, in 1926, he married Pauline Buckeridge. Pauline, Guy's mother, was born and brought up in South Africa. Her father was from Devonshire, while her mother's family were 1820 settlers and ostrich farmers in the South. As a young woman,

Pauline Buckeridgs with Donkey cart. South Africa

Pauline developed her own car-hire business, with herself and another girl as drivers. During the first World War she drove ambulances in France. Later, she came to Kenya for further adventure, and met Hugh. After they were married Hugh joined the Colonial Administration, which meant that he spent much of his time posted to distant places including the Northern Frontier District, which was out of bounds at that time to the families of civil servants. So Pauline would take Guy and his sisters, Anne and Deirdre, to visit ranching friends from where they could attend school. When Guy was six he rode a donkey to lessons with neighbours. His father's leaves were eagerly looked forward to and meanwhile Guy practiced his riding and shooting. When the whole family were at Kajiado, where Hugh was D.C. for a while before the Second World War, he and Guy did wildebeeste shooting for the Game Department (Guy being only 12 at the time). Later, Hugh became British Consul in Southern Ethiopia, and at that time Pauline bought a small farm called Springhill, at

Guy ploughing at Springhill with Somali stallion

Guy (front) going to school with the Webbers, Mua Hills 1936

Limuru, not far from Nairobi, which Guy helped his mother to run in the holidays – and there he kept his first cows. Earlier he had attended Pembroke House School at Gilgil, and during the farming years he was at the Prince of Wales School in Nairobi.

When the Second World War broke out Hugh Grant formed his own company of irregular soldiers, Grant's Irregulars, with whom he fought in the Ethiopian campaign. By then, Guy was expected to enter Eton, where his father had been. In 1944, though the war was still in progress, Guy travelled on his own, aged fifteen, down the Nile. He met a missionary on the steam-boat who helped him embark on a troop ship from Cairo. Safely arrived in Scotland in spite of 'U' boats in the Atlantic, he went to stay at his father's family home, Knockie, in Inverness-shire.

From Knockie, Guy took himself to Eton to sit the entrance exam. But farming at Limuru was insufficient preparation for Latin exams at Eton, and he failed. An uncle suggested he try Stowe, so to Stowe he went (again on his own) to interview the Headmaster. J. F. Roxburgh, impressed by Guy's initiative and independence, enrolled him at once without an examination. Guy worked hard for the two years he was at Stowe, spending his holidays at Knockie where he helped on the farm and kept the larder supplied with venison. After matriculating at seventeen and a half years old, Guy immediately

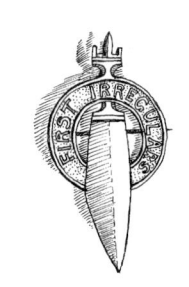

Badge of the Irregulars

SOME HISTORY AND THE LAND   3

volunteered for the army, joining the Cameron Highlanders. At this time Springhill farm in Kenya was sold and Guy's father re-joined the Administration as District Commissioner at Narok. Hugh had been one of ten children, five boys and five girls, but two of his brothers did not return from the war. Now, Guy received the news of his own father's tragic death. He had been speared in the back by a Maasai after a disagreement over a black bull, during a time when it was Government policy to buy Maasai cattle to feed the troops.

Knockie

After transferring to the Argylls Guy saw active service in Palestine during the final six months of 1948 when the British kept a peace-keeping mission in that country. Later, he took a degree in agriculture at Cambridge University. Returning to Kenya in 1953, he worked on different farms and ranches, and for the Government, until independence. At that time, when many were leaving the country, Guy saw the opportunity to acquire his own land. He leased grazing for some steers bought with an Agricultural Finance Corporation loan, and with the proceeds from the fattened beasts he took over the Osborne's Land Bank loan, payed the difference between that and the price of the land, and El Karama was his. It was indeed an answer to prayer, for Guy had always dreamt of, and worked towards, owning his own ranch in Laikipia.

Zebras at Ol Mara dam

Neighbours, the Barkers, soon left the country for Australia, and Guy managed to add their four thousand acre section of land to the eight thousand acres of El Karama, which made the ranch a more useful size. This land is called 'Ol Mara', meaning 'striped' or 'spotted' in Maasai.

Ol Mara was well named, for long cloud shadows brindle the bleached tawny of its rolling land in dry weather, and the soft terre-vert of its grass after rain. Much of it is bush-stippled, and it is crossed by three main gullies which carry seasonal rain water to the river Uaso Nyiro along its western boundary. There is a dam scooped in the ancient red earth of Ol Mara, upon whose wall tumbles wild ipomoea, smothered in pink trumpet flowers in the mornings. It is shallow enough for Black-winged stilts and avocets to wade; not large enough for more than one pair of Egyptian geese to raise their seven or eight white-spotted goslings there. Families and loose coagulations of zebras wander down to the dam and toss water with their muzzles before drinking, making small conversational, doglike whines to each other continuously. The slopes around the dam are worn bare by the hooves of creatures both wild and domestic, which constantly resort there while the dam holds water. But in the dry seasons the water evaporates, leaving algae-varnished polygons of dried mud divided by deep cracks.

The sky of Ol Mara is often crossed by the smudges of fast-moving flocks of birds, changing shape but not cohesion, until suddenly a flock contracts into the crown of a tree like a mass of iron filings to a strong magnet, and a sound of twittering breaks out. Some of the trees are decorated with the golden fruit of weaver's nests; hanging balls of grasses, with the entrances underneath to discourage snakes and other bird-eaters. However, the African harrier-hawk often hangs from the nests by one long, yellow leg, flapping, while feeling double-jointedly inside with the other leg for nestlings. Gabar goshawks tear open the nests from above, a pair sometimes being responsible for the total breeding failure of a weaver colony.

At the northern end of Ol Mara is the Game Plain, a high, domed ridge from which one can see, all around, distant mountains, hills and kopjes, with the long, sloping shoulders and pointed glacier-encrusted peaks of Mt. Kenya to the east. Swifts, martins and swallows sweep low over the windy grass, and always there are wild animals. Grévy's zebras turn to swivel their radar-disk ears, and herds of oryx canter smoothly away as soon as one trespasses inside the exactly determined point at which they must always flee. The largest herds of Thomson's gazelles live there, and on the lee slope of the ridge is a big *boma*, built to contain cows and calves at night.

Across the river from Ol Mara there is a high, rocky plateau fringed with combretum trees. The first European to live on this

Gabar Gosshawks (Melanistic and normal)

Weaver nests

Pair of Harrier-hawks

place was named Fochs, when it was known on Ordinance Survey maps as Fochs's farm. Later, it was inherited by his daughter, who

Beisa Oryx

married a Jauss. When Mr. Jauss died tragically, having accidentally drunk a poisonous dip sample which was in a beer bottle, Mrs. Jauss and her son, Mike, continued alone at the farm. When he was twelve years old, Mike would ride to Nanyuki once a week on a bicycle to do the chores – a round trip of about sixty miles. They kept cattle and pigs, and although life must have been hard for them, Mike always loved the place. Eventually the Jausses moved to the coast, when Fochs's farm was sold to Mr. Gichunju, a Kikuyu butcher, as a holding-ground for butchers' stock. Sometimes the grazing was let to Inga and Ole Jacobsen, Danes of Nanyuki, who called it 'Klipspringer Farm'. Inga loved the place, saying she always felt well there, in spite of the crippling arthritis she suffered permanently. She told us how the rocky plateau attracted lightning. The house, at that time, was already ruined, and the Jacobsens would camp in it when they visited to check on their cattle. When Gichunju died, the land went to his brother, Nderitu.

Guy had always thought that this plateau would be a useful addition to El Karama, and I loved it for its beauty – but to own it seemed an impossible dream. In 1990 we heard that it was up for sale, to be divided into five-acre plots. We were sad, for if it were sold to small-holders they would not be able to make a living, and the land would be turned to the equivalent of desert. Prospective buyers came from afar, five large buses and six crowded 'matatus' (taxis) passing, astonishingly (for we are far from main roads), through our farmyard one day; but the land, owing to its rockiness, remained unsold. Then, suddenly and unexpectedly, I inherited a legacy from a cousin. It was enough! We applied for Land Board permission to buy the land. This was granted in July 1991 and after seemingly endless legal proceedings had been gone through, the title deeds were made out and the 2,300 acres belonged to our three grown-up children, Laria, Isabella and Murray. We named it Combretum, after the trees so characteristic of the land.

After rain these trees are covered with new spring-green leaves which, later, turn heavier and darker, and are finally shed with the dry weather to reveal strangely twisted branches and rough, knobbly

Turtle

trunks. Against these, elephants like to rub. The Uaso Nyiro river runs along part of this land and is joined by a smaller, seasonal river, the Suguroi, which follows the Southern march. The vegetation of Combretum is unusual and interesting, and some of its trees and flowers do not grow on El Karama. In most parts of this land the iron-hard rock of its volcanic foundation is exposed in irregular brown expanses and ridges, on which are rock pools during the rains. Shallow areas of earth covered with stones and growing sparse grass, border these pitted sheets of rock; and on the escarpments which edge the plateau huge boulders, the size of double-storey buildings, form a jumble in which live hyraxes, klipspringers and numerous leopards. To the north is a tract of deeper soil covered with thicker grass and an extensive woodland of whistling-thorns.

There is a rock pan on the high central plateau of Combretum which, after rain, flashes a reflection of the sky to passing waterfowl and waders, which come down to rest and feed there. Around it, the curly pink and white trumpets of Pyjama lilies appear briefly before being eaten as a delicacy by insects, tortoises and eland. A water weed with tiny flowers sometimes scents the air almost over-poweringly with honey, while on every flat rock jutting from the shallow water sit turtles, occasionally three (once we saw four) stacked one on top of the other; and the short-cropped turf of the little upland around the pan is studded with small wild flowers. But in dry weather you would not know that the water, turtles, flowers and birds had ever been there.

There are many small springs on Combretum, and one we know of is to be found under three rocks not far above a track along the river. Below it a streamlet has made a winding course for itself amongst the stones, bright green with mosses and algae, thick with sedges and grass, although in dry weather there is only a slight dampness on the ground to mark it. Around the rocks is a bay of vegetation, frequented by baby frogs and dragonflies. Under the rocks lies a pool only a few inches deep, of a strange blue and milky opaqueness, common to all the ground water of Combretum, which has always puzzled us. Behind the spring you come upon winding and braided tracks made by animals coming down to the river to drink, worn bare by zebra, eland, elephant and cattle. Follow these paths upwards and you come again to the ubiquitous rock, and eventually to a corrie surrounded on three sides by higher rocks on which stand combretum trees. Out of the hard ground of this corrie grow many bulbs of Boophone disticha, the 'ox-killer', their glaucous leaves opening in beautiful, flat fans. These plants bear heads of red flowers which later develop into globes of spokes, nearly two feet in diameter, each spoke carrying at its end round shiny seeds. As the ground becomes bare in the dry weather, these heads detach and

Klipspringers

Pyjama lily (*Crinum sp.*)

Monsonia ovata

SOME HISTORY AND THE LAND 7

tumble along in the wind like giant spiders, dropping seeds as they go.

From the corrie of the ox-killers one can see out through a filigree of branches across the undulating plains of El Karama to the mountain, while far below to the right is the old Combretum house on a grey-green meadow under the escarpment. If you climb on above the corrie you come out onto a flat plateau of rock, the shallow earthy pans of which are filled with the rhizomes of the graceful cream-coloured Candida gladiolus (Gladiolus ukambanensis), which flowers everywhere there after good rains.

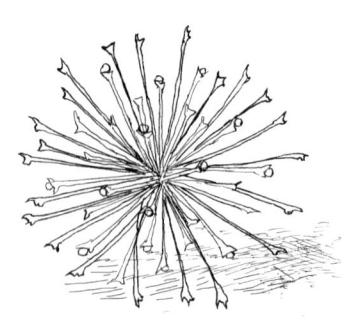

Candida gladiolus

Boöphone seedhead (nearly 2 foot diameter)

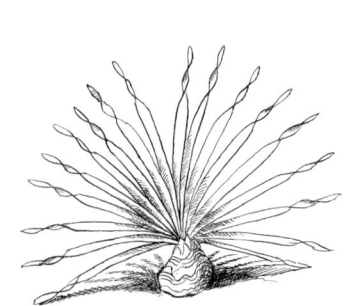

Boöphone disticha

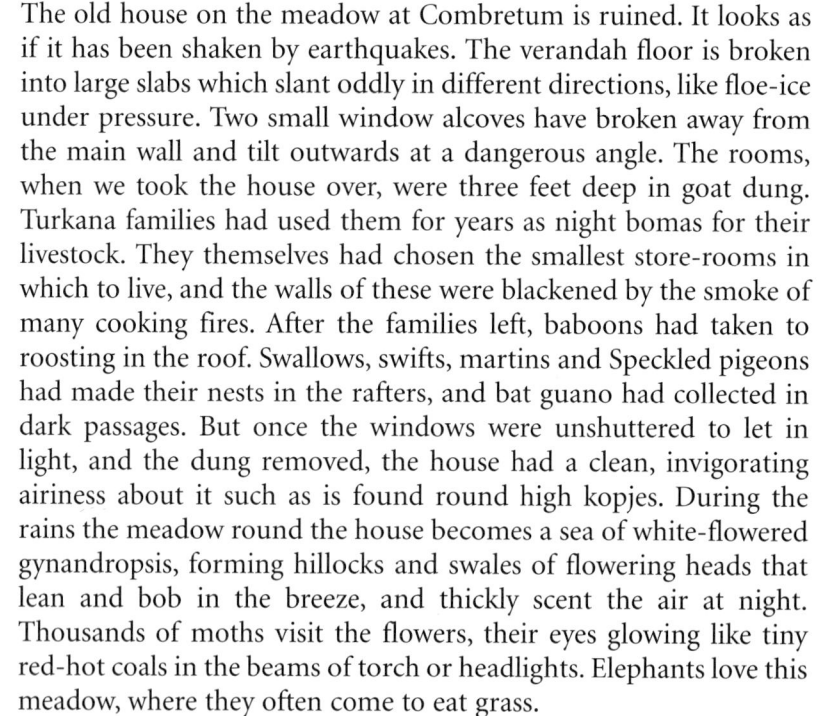

The old house on the meadow at Combretum is ruined. It looks as if it has been shaken by earthquakes. The verandah floor is broken into large slabs which slant oddly in different directions, like floe-ice under pressure. Two small window alcoves have broken away from the main wall and tilt outwards at a dangerous angle. The rooms, when we took the house over, were three feet deep in goat dung. Turkana families had used them for years as night bomas for their livestock. They themselves had chosen the smallest store-rooms in which to live, and the walls of these were blackened by the smoke of many cooking fires. After the families left, baboons had taken to roosting in the roof. Swallows, swifts, martins and Speckled pigeons had made their nests in the rafters, and bat guano had collected in dark passages. But once the windows were unshuttered to let in light, and the dung removed, the house had a clean, invigorating airiness about it such as is found round high kopjes. During the rains the meadow round the house becomes a sea of white-flowered gynandropsis, forming hillocks and swales of flowering heads that lean and bob in the breeze, and thickly scent the air at night. Thousands of moths visit the flowers, their eyes glowing like tiny red-hot coals in the beams of torch or headlights. Elephants love this meadow, where they often come to eat grass.

The views from the front and sides of the house are vast; expanses of bush and cloud shadow, hills and mountain, rocks and the river valley; all steeped in light as clear and astringent as gin, under the

Gynandropsis gynandra

Convolvulaceae

Ipomoea

Sept '95

May '92

Ipomoea hildebrandtii megaënsis

Rubiaceae.
Pavetta teitana

Hiacinth-scented.

May '92.

July '92.

Pavetta at Combretum falls

Looking towards Mt. Kenya from the garden (dry weather)

The ranch house

The El Karama lines 1998

Mangoes in the Orchard

Nyctaginaceae.   *Bougainvillea.*

April '92

Looking North

Looking north from the garden

Bignoniaceae
Spathodea campanulata.   Nandi Flame tree.
Native to Kenya.

May 1991.

Orchard gate.

Nandi Flame in the garden

Red-billed fire-finch
(*Lagonosticta senegala*).

Nest in hoya plant,
varandah ceiling. '95.

THE HOUSE AT COMBRETUM

From the broken verandah, clouds like serried ships at sea
Grow smaller with distance, are torn by swifts.
Through frameless window, hanging door, the antiseptic air is free,
And moans and hums beneath the creaking roof, and through rifts
In the corners of walls and floor.

Scoured clean as sun and air, bare as a bone, as dry,
The house reminds me of empty canvas, a white page
On which my mind can paint ideas, imprint, then fly.
The feeling is of birth, in spite of the house's age.
Outside, chirrup-whistling swifts drive circuits in the air.

From empty windows, brindled bush and sun-reflecting grass
Lead, behind, to Combretum's rocky edge (full of rock-pools after showers).
During the day eland graze; at dawn elephants pass.
The lawn of the house: star-grass, sedge,
Light, and dancing wild flowers.

profound dome of the sky. At night the sky seems bigger from the house than from anywhere else, even at sea – because of the altitude. There are no rocks, hills, trees or other buildings very near, and in the dark the earth seems shrunk to a basin around the house. The vastness above is peppered with stars so thickly that in places they form nimbuses of dim silver, while Adeboran, Antares, Sirius, the Pleiades, and countless others whose names I never knew, blaze their freezing fire; and over them all, the ancient patterns of the constellations are imprinted: Orion, the Great Bear, Taurus, and the Southern Cross. The lights of Nanyuki, thirty miles distant, which we thought might be intrusive from here, are of no significance; merely yellower, dimmer stars at the bottom of the sky.

Once Combretum had become part of El Karama, we decided to explore the length of the Suguroi river, for the part of it we had seen already was intriguing. The river is flanked by long, slanting benches of rock, in the cracks of which grows a little shrub called Resurrection bush, or Turkana tea. This shrub appears quite dead until almost immediately after a shower of rain, when suddenly it is covered with tiny, fan-like leaves of brilliant shiny green. Between the rocks grow combretum and canthium trees. The river itself, in truth no more than a stream, sometimes slides over long slopes of smooth rock, sparkling in the sun; or lies in cool pools under the yellow-thorns and figs, the green chianti-bottle nests of Vitteline masked weavers suspended above. Dragon flies, electric blue, orange, red, yellow, green and brown, dart over the surface, settling momentarily on waterside rocks or overhanging vegetation. Under rocks on the slopes above the river live small, brown scorpions – shy and surprisingly inoffensive. We were surprised when we found these scorpions for, being at an altitude of almost 6,000 feet, Combretum is higher than the rest of El Karama, where they have not yet been seen. In the dry weather the Suguroi often dries up completely, exposing the strangely varnished rocks of its bed.

The day of exploration was grey and windy with a light drizzle. The rocks were shining like the backs of sounding whales in the Atlantic, and the Suguroi was foaming in white lace over the rock-slides of its course. At length we came to a crescent-shaped pool beneath an ancient, twisted fig tree. From the pool's surface a pair of Black river ducks took off, and flying the length of it, beat out into space where the pool suddenly ended. We had arrived at a terrific vertical fault over which the little Suguroi fell in seeming slow motion, feathering in the air; while the sound of the water shattering on the rocks below made a hushing sound which came and went rhythmically with the pulsing of the water. Under the huge red and black rocks of the cliffs were caves and caverns, and in the air beneath us Scarce swifts and Rock martins swept dizzily to and fro.

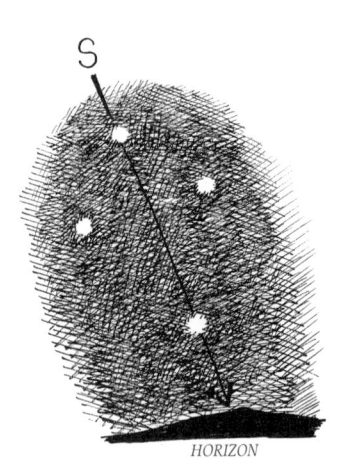

10 ON A KENYA RANCH

On the edge of the cliffs grew shrubs that I had never seen before, bearing clusters of green, hyacinth-scented flowers; and wild bees flew in and out of a cleft below the lip of the falls. Under the rocks at the base of these falls is a cave in which, we heard later, 'freedom

Black River ducks

fighters' had hidden during the Mau Mau period of Kenya's history. In seasons of rain the Suguroi in spate flings a stupendous weight of tawny water over the falls, the roar of which, when the wind is right, can be heard from miles away; and one can see the cream-coloured wall of foam continuously and hypnotically moving downwards, from far off. Yet we had not known previously that these falls existed!

One afternoon some time after our discovery of the falls, when Murray was throwing small pebbles over the cliff in order to hear the echoing ping of their landing, he called out suddenly 'A leopard!'. A big leopard, disturbed by the stones, was climbing swiftly up a gigantic boulder at the side of the falls as easily as if his feet were soled with Velcro, his muscles bulging and rippling beneath the closely set black rosettes on the green-gold velvet of his skin. Climbing down the rocks above the leopard but unable yet to see it, was a friend. We shouted a warning. He stood still and slowly raised his head. Just then the leopard saw him and at little more than ten feet away, veered to one side and bounded out of view along a vegetation-covered ledge. We could trace his progress by a series of bolting hyraxes.

Visitors to El Karama often tell us that we live in a garden of Eden; and so we do. But they cannot know of the work that goes into looking after the ranch and how many obstacles must be overcome if it is to continue, and not disappear like mist in the morning, as so many other Edens have done.

Vitelline masked weaver

Leopard climbing rock

Rock hyraxes

SOME HISTORY AND THE LAND 11

SELECTING STOCK

The dogs - white, brindled, gold -
Nested in grass,
Watch the work with cattle.
Bulls, red, move about
Or crop the verdant green.
An horizon behind melts
With rain.
New blossom on the trees
Fills dampened air with scent.
People move slow,
Thoughtfully selecting stock.
And I watch from the fence.

It has been like that
From long ago;
But not for many, now.
Time - tamed to the slow
Movement of a bull,
To cropping of grass,
Changing of sky from sun to rain -
Is not allowed.
But here, time still moves thus,
Like blossom growing on a tree;
As I stand by the fence.

The Men and Livestock

One evening we were on Toru, a ridge above Ol Mara dam, watching a concentration of wild animals coming to drink at the caerulean oval of water, when we heard an incongruous bray. A file of donkeys came earnestly hurrying into view, moving towards the Game Plain which is some distance beyond the dam. It was already dusk and we knew the donkeys should not have been there, and alone. Hurrying to collect a herdsman from the nearest boma, we drove to the, then unoccupied, boma on the flanks of the Game Plain. Our donkeys, obviously pleased at having reached 'safety' before dark, had put themselves away inside it. Kibon, a Pokot, said he would return them at once to the bull boma where they should have been. This boma was on the other side of the ranch, and it was now dark. Having said goodbye, we were driving back along the track when a herd of zebras galloped across in front of us, bright in the headlights; and in their midst were the donkeys. Immediately behind them, at full stretch but keeping up well, came Kibon! We

Bella and Guy inspecting Boran cows

House herd coming into back yard - evening

waited while he regathered his spooked charges. He said cheerfully that he would spend the night at the bull boma. He laughed at me when I suggested he would need a blanket, and set off through the cold and windy darkness in shirt and waist-cloth, to cross miles of bush in which were probably buffalo, possibly elephants, surely puff-adders; herding before him eight nervous donkeys. But to him it was all in a day's work, and unremarkable.

Because the ranch employs people of different tribes, they speak Swahili in order to communicate with each other; for each of the many tribes and peoples of Kenya have their own language. Some also speak English. Most of the men employed here have their own plots of land (shambas) or flocks and herds, in the part of country from which they come. Wives and families usually stay at home to look after these shambas and livestock, and children attend school from there. The men go home on leave, and wives accompanied by children visit their menfolk here, often for weeks at a time. Many

Wives and children arrived in Nanyuki

employees have worked on the ranch for over twenty years, and are truly part of the ranch community. Because in the past wages and the cost of living have been fairly low, we have been able to employ many people, in a manner that is no longer possible in other parts of the world. This has provided a living for many families. But with increasing wages and costs of living in Kenya, it is becoming more difficult to manage in this old-fashioned way, and the time may soon come when El Karama will be unable to help so many people.

Sometimes men walk for days in order to reach the ranch to ask for work, but new recruits are usually brought by employees from their home areas, for then they have a sense of responsibility for the behaviour of protegés. However, we receive many applications for work by letter and these are often phrased amusingly with an inventive, sometimes accidentally almost poetic, use of English (for English is not their first, or even second, language). 'Dear Employer, to start with is to say a word of hullo from this edge of the globe' or: 'Sir kindly Soreward, I am here at this moment of trueth trying to delight my gratitudes to you, Sir. The cardinal matter for writing this

Sickle

document are as forels . . .' etcetera. Some letters are more worldly-wise and fluent as this application for the post of driver illustrates: 'I have a wide experience in cars. I am dynamic, self motivated, energetic and result orientated. I am thirty five years old, regenerated and married . . . Sir, I believe I have the necessary drive to meet my duties . . . looking forward to a positive feedback. . .'

Everyone who works on the ranch is expected to be flexible, doing not only his own main work but anything else that needs to be done, and standing in for the sick or for those on leave. Thus a clerk will often be out with the cattle, helping at the yards or treating sick animals. The driver may be collecting firewood, digging rocks or murram, or decarbonising the pump engine at the river. Horsemen may find themselves herding, or mending fences; and so on with every employee excepting the herdsmen themselves. The general labour and herdsmen's assistants may be set to digging fence post holes, mixing salt and minerals for the cattle, herding the hospital animals and cutting feed for them, digging rubbish holes or 'long drops', re-mudding houses, thatching, moving bomas, digging road ditches, clearing boundaries and fire breaks, loading or unloading lorries, cutting hay or Bonar grass, looking for lost animals, or any of the seemingly endless number and variety of jobs that always need doing on a ranch.

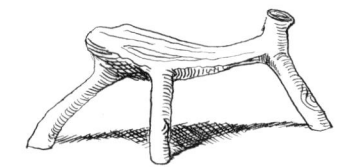

At six-thirty each morning everyone at headquarters gathers at the hot water system fire outside the garden gate, to stand by its warmth or squat on rustic stools as they drink steaming tins of sweet, milky tea, which has been brewed by the night watchman. Here the day's work plan, worked out the previous evening, is read out so that everyone knows what his tasks are to be. By seven o'clock they are away to start work.

Young assistant

Rustic stool

Herdsmen's shelters at cow boma, Oryx Plain

Coming to work at El Karama is sometimes the first time the men have left their homes. Recently a young Pokot was wondering out loud if anyone lived beyond Mt. Kenya, which looked so huge and far away. He was surprised when told that Meru and Kikuyu people lived beyond and around it. 'But no-one would ever go up there' he said with conviction, indicating the peak. When our elder daughter, Laria, told him she herself had been up as far as one of the big patches of snow he could see, he was both astonished and excited.

The Pokots have a reputation for fierceness and our men have more than once recovered stolen livestock from thieves as it was being hurried across El Karama from other ranches. They are tough people. Our son asked a Pokot, who for some reason had gone without food all day, if he was not hungry. The young man, looking at him in surprise, answered 'Why should I be hungry after only one day without food?'. Sometimes, in his home country, he told Murray, the men go for weeks with only a little milk each day. The names of some of the Pokot herdsmen whom we have employed still ring in my mind for they have particularly musical names: Lottaboi and Laut, Akarel and Gollikat, Limurion, Lopotan and Lopiok.

Our herdsmen are normally recruited from Pokot, Meru, Tharakan, Somali or Boran people, who are used to living all year round with stock and sleeping in shelters at night. They are able to be out all day, sometimes in punishing heat, in hot dry winds, or

Pokot sandals

Bull herdsman resting

heavy soaking rainstorms. Nights are often cold, for the ranch is at an altitude of 5,700 feet; Combretum being even higher.

The herdsmen of the ranch are responsible, of course, for its wealth. Falling asleep under a tree in the heat of the day, very easy to do when drugged by the sun and the wind, or failing to notice that two bulls are about to fight, can have serious consequences. For if cattle wander off and are not found before nightfall they may be killed and eaten by lions or hyaenas. During fights a bull sometimes breaks a leg, and then has to be destroyed. This has

Milking

actually happened to a number of our bulls; including 'Makala' – one of the best. It is surprisingly easy for cattle to blunder into elephants in thick bush during the day, and the herdsman for his

Returning to the boma

own safety has also to keep a wary eye out for buffaloes. And if he is not diligent, drought-weakened cows may stick in the mud of nearly-empty dams or fall into the river and not be able to get out.

The cattle are let out of the bomas to start grazing early in the morning and care is taken where they graze during the day, or they may quickly lose condition, or even die, when fodder is scarce during dry weather or droughts. A good herdsman notices at once when an animal begins to be unwell and makes sure it is treated quickly, as early treatment often makes the difference between life and death. Notice is taken of which cows are served, when, and by which bull, so that the information can be entered on the cow's record card. Of course, the arrival of a herd of cows at water must not coincide there with the arrival of the bulls, or these records may become muddled! The herdsman knows when a cow is due to calve and is ready to help the newborn back to the herd, and if it is not strong enough to walk with its mother (which it usually is), then Mother and calf must be taken to the homestead to be looked after there.

Herdsmen keep contact with the cattle during the day through a series of melodious and varied whistles – 'hurrying' whistles, 'slowing' whistles, 'calming' and 'order-keeping' whistles. Sometimes one may hear a lone voice raised in song, the cadences sweet with contentment and made beautiful and somehow meaningful by distance and the lovely surroundings, as a herdsman wanders slowly through the bush with his charges.

Each evening the animals are counted into their bomas and the calves of cows that are to be milked in the morning are separated and put into a small enclosure inside the main one, so that they do not suck from their mothers during the night. Salt box lids are removed so that the cattle can take what they need, and put back again in the morning to prevent giraffes and zebras finishing the salt

Milk churn

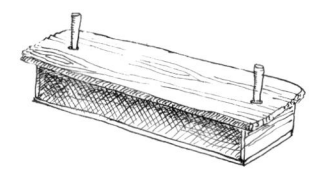

Salt box

THE MEN AND LIVESTOCK 17

during the day. Milking is begun in the cold before dawn, when the first colour creeps into the sky behind the silent mountain. The milk, in churns, is then loaded onto donkeys and transported to headquarters, accompanied by the herdsman's assistant.

The dairy (with Melda)

As we live too far from a market and there are insurmountable problems with transportation of the milk to town, while green grass lasts the surplus is separated in a small dairy behind the house. Every morning the sound of the separating machine is heard, quiet to begin with, as the stiff handle is slowly turned by hand. At each revolution a bell 'tings' and gradually the tings come closer together as the sound of the separator gets louder and higher. Soon it is like a small jet aeroplane and the operator's voice rises as he tries to make his conversation heard; and is answered by cheerful shouts from others. When the bell stops ringing the handle is turning fast enough, and cream begins to come from one spout while skimmed milk gushes from another, foaming into a churn below. Some of the skimmed milk is mixed with the horses' feeds, and some is given to the poultry to boost egg production, after everyone has taken what they want of it. The cream is stored in a charcoal 'fridge' built outside, with double walls of wire-netting. The space between these walls is filled with charcoal which, when wet, causes evaporation to make the inside of the 'fridge' cool.

Butter is made early in the mornings when it is still cool, by stirring the cream with a wooden paddle in a big bowl until the yellow butter-grains appear, floating in butter-milk. When it has solidified it is washed many times in rain water, and beaten into cubes with wooden butter-pats. Surplus butter is clarified to preserve it, by heating in a large pan on an outside fire. It must not burn or boil over – both can happen easily and suddenly – for if it burns the flavour and colour is spoilt, and if it boils over the whole pan will ignite in a flash. Froth from the surface is skimmed off and the clear

Donkey pack saddle for carrying milk churns

liquid butter poured into buckets, where it sets. This 'ghee' keeps fresh indefinitely and food cooked with it is crisp, tasty and golden. Ghee and butter are periodically taken to Nanyuki for sale to Somali hotels and local shops, or issued to the ranch workers in dry weather.

After a day of general labour, an assistant herdsman returns with the donkeys through the golden light of late afternoon to the boma, bringing water in the churns, salt for the cattle, or stores for the men. He prepares the simple evening meal, usually of maize-meal (*ugali*) washed down with fresh milk, and milky, sweet tea (*chai*), so that it is ready when the cattle are in. And the dog which will have accompanied the cattle all day, is fed. At night the herdsmen, even while sleeping, are ready to respond to this dog's warning of lion, hyaena or elephant, and react appropriately, at the same time soothing frightened animals lest they stampede. One man at each of the eight or so bomas on the ranch is responsible for, and able to use, a shot gun. This is for self defence and to deter thieves, as well as for frightening off wild animals.

The different herds are brought to the homestead on specific days for dipping, and the herdsmen will help at monthly de-horning and ear-marking (when calves are seven weeks old), and at weaning and castration (at eight months old), and at the selection of heifers to go to the cow herd for breeding (at approximately two years old). So they need to know, individually, every animal in their herds. Bulls with the breeding herd are changed over, on average, every month.

In view of all this it is perhaps surprising how many good herdsmen there have been, and are, on the ranch. They are not, of course, angels, and there is sometimes the temptation to buy *chang'aa*, a deadly home-brew, from 'across the fence'. One herdsman passed out, another was rendered incapable of counting his goats, while yet another was caught, having deserted his cattle, spending the night off the ranch in the company of his shotgun (a heinous crime). Some years ago, a temporary horseman who had ridden direct to his source of supply instead of on his scheduled patrol of the cattle bomas, remained in the bush asleep on his back until found by the search party which set out as soon as his riderless steed appeared in the stableyard. Occasionally cattle are abandoned while the herdsmen follow a bird, the Greater honey-guide, to a wild bee-hive in order to break out the honey with the help of smoke from smouldering cow pats, and a fire was once started on El Karama in this way. Sometimes honey is stolen from our own bee-hives, but the thief there is more often a honey-badger (Ratel) than the two-legged kind.

As there is usually quite a large number of people on the ranch, hardly a day goes by without requests for medicine or first aid, and

Ghee simmering

Charcoal fridge

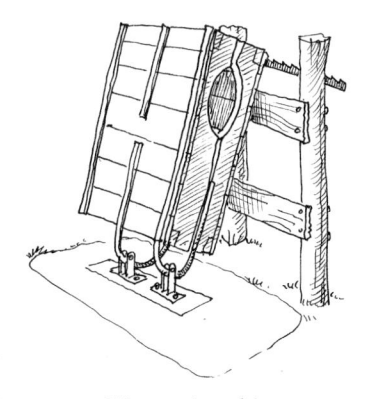

Weaner 'crush'

THE MEN AND LIVESTOCK 19

EAR MARKING

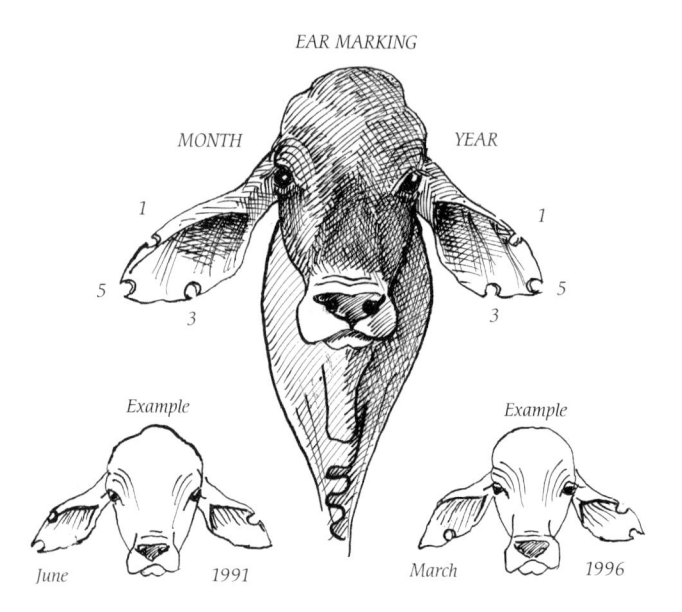

MONTH · YEAR

Example June 1991

Example March 1996

it has been my task to administer these using simple medicines – Panadol, vitamin C, cough mixture, farm liniment etc., and a useful book called 'Where there is no doctor'. At times it can be a frightening responsibility. One cannot send everyone with small problems to see a doctor, for then a car would be on the road nearly every day: an impracticability when the distance, the roughness of the road, and the cost of vehicle maintenance are considered. It is comforting to know there is the Flying Doctor service for emergencies.

A mother brought her baby to me saying she was sure he was very ill, but though he seemed listless, he was clear-eyed with no temperature. I thought there was nothing seriously wrong. But the mother insisted. She had lost her previous baby at about the same age, and his symptoms had been as vague. I told her we would watch him and if he grew worse would do something about it. But, half an hour later, a feeling came to me suddenly and strongly that the baby must be sent to Nanyuki immediately. We hurried to arrange it, and our daughter, Laria, drove them in. When mother and child arrived at the hospital the baby was admitted at once and given blood transfusions. The doctor said that if they had been an hour later the baby would have died. He had sickle-cell anaemia, exacerbated by malaria suppressed by the sickle-cells, and his red blood count was critically low.

Because cooking is often done on an open fire with three stones for an hearth, and karais (metal bowls) of boiling water are left, perforce, where children can reach them, burns and scalds are quite common. A little child actually sat down in a karai of boiling water, and after an initial visit to the doctor, I had to dress this awful scald for weeks.

'Karai' with rustic spirtle and spoon

One afternoon a young man came running to the house saying he had been bitten by a snake. Though he was naturally concerned, he was not suffering from shock. From his lucid description of its appearance and of the way it had hung on and had to be shaken off, we thought the snake had been an Olive grass snake, and therefore only mildly venomous. He confirmed this after being shown an illustration. But we could not be certain so he was sent to see a doctor immediately. A fang which had broken off in his foot was removed, but otherwise he suffered no ill effects.

Olive grass-snake

Apart from occasional emergencies – the goring of a herdsman by a buffalo, a finger sliced off by the road-grader, a blood clot on the brain resulting from a fall during fire-fighting, twisted intestines, or ruptured appendices (one of the latter was suffered by our son, and I myself got a twisted intestine) – the daily sick parade is usually

The road grader

hum-drum. Headaches, small cuts, intestinal worms, thorns, kicks from cows, injured 'leg fingers' (toes), colds, coughs and 'loose joints' are the usual complaints.

The first we hear of illness is usually by note from the ranch clerk, whose English, though often amusing, is invariably better and more adventurous than my Swahili. This description came in one morning: 'The problem is when he goes in grass nothing comes out. The stomach gives melodious sounds, and he can stand but just for short minutes'. Next day's note reported that 'The melodies are now reduced to a certain degree'. A woman with vomiting and diarrhoea was reported better after drinking the 'dehydrated water given her yesterday'. This was a relief, as: 'The master (husband) is kindly asking for a help in away to make his wife see the doctor immediately to make her ends meet'. Veterinary notes are sent, too, and to our amusement, a cow was reported to have 'stepped on her bosom'.

There used to be an occasional rush to Nanyuki in the middle of the night with a wife about to give birth, and once a baby was born in the car. Sometimes it was left too late altogether and a mother would have her baby on the ranch – usually without ill effects although conditions are very far indeed from sterile at the bomas, where babies were occasionally born. But nowadays we try to make sure that women go home three months before a baby is due.

Malaria is commonly suffered by people returning from leave in other parts of the country, but it is difficult to tell from a bout of 'flu without a blood test. As it is dangerous to misdiagnose, there is often the dilemma of whether to send a patient to town at once, or not. We used to be able to treat malaria at home but as it is now resistant to drugs which formerly were effective and easy to use, trips to town with the sick are more frequent than they used to be.

Guy branding Boran heifers

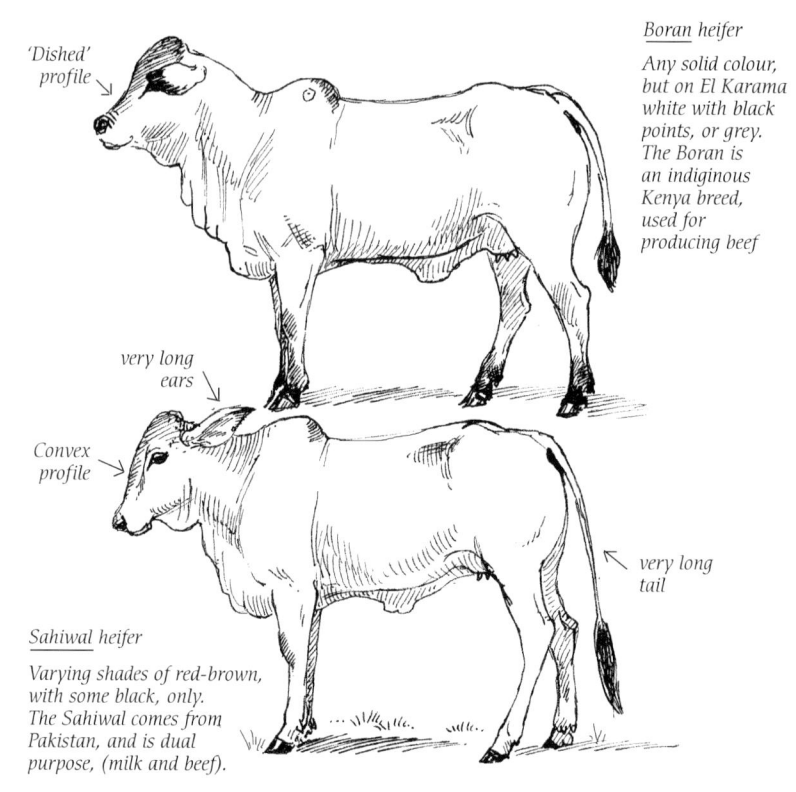

'Dished' profile

Boran heifer
Any solid colour, but on El Karama white with black points, or grey. The Boran is an indigenous Kenya breed, used for producing beef

very long ears

Convex profile

very long tail

Sahiwal heifer
Varying shades of red-brown, with some black, only. The Sahiwal comes from Pakistan, and is dual purpose, (milk and beef).

The two breeds of El Karama cattle (to compare)

Guy's first cattle on El Karama were held in partnership; a motley collection of cross-breds; speckled, pied and parti-coloured, some with horns and some without; their various ancestry showing in their widely varying forms. With white, grey and eland-coloured cows, Guy ran well-bred Boran bulls: the Boran being a breed of humped cattle originally developed by the Boran people of northern Kenya (the classic Boran animal being white with black points). Cows of all other colours he put with bulls of the red Sahiwal breed, from Pakistan. Each year his cattle increased and improved in appearance and eventually they were good enough to register as purebred and pedigree Borans and Sahiwals, and were sold mainly

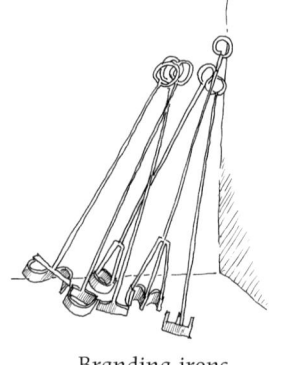

Branding irons

as breeding stock. For a time the two breeds were kept side by side, but this necessitated much recording, bookwork and extra man-power and the ranch was not really large enough to justify keeping two separate breeds. So, one year of financial difficulty, the Boran herd, result of twenty-seven years of selection and loving care, was sold. Guy felt that the Sahiwals had an advantage over the Borans: their ability to produce quantities of milk while retaining their beef-building conformation and resilience in hard ranch conditions. For whilst there is no tougher breed than the Boran, whose con-formation is perhaps stockier than that of the Sahiwal, they can produce little milk more than that needed to feed their calves. While the Boran can legitimately be almost any colour, the Sahiwals' glossy hides reflect the sun in shades only of golden red, bright bay and rich mahogany; all with black tail-tufts and hooves. The bulls have great dark humps and black-smudged shoulders and quarters, while around each black nose is a ring of mealy-coloured fur.

Sahiwal bull

Sahiwal calves

A curious characteristic of the Sahiwals is their quietness. A herd may come to the yards and leave again without one being aware of it from the house – except during activities such as weaning (when all cattle are noisy) – whereas the Borans would bellow continuously, sounding from a distance like the ebb and flow of surf on a shingly beach. Sahiwal bulls do not call with the ringing bellows of Northern cattle, designed to be heard through thick forests; neither do they sound like the African Zebu beasts, but make strange indrawn groans ending in explosive grunts, often extraordinarily like the call made by hunting tigers. Why this should have developed in cattle coming from a land where tigers must once have been common I have wondered, but perhaps the similarity is only super-ficial. The Sahiwal, like the Jersey, is often said to be fierce. But as Guy has always selected for calm, friendly temperament, rigorously culling unsuitable characters, our herd is very peaceful towards humans. It always surprises me how quickly such selection can take effect.

Although cattle are the most important of the domestic animals

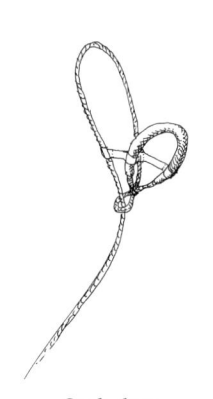

Ox-halter

THE MEN AND LIVESTOCK 23

Carrying manure (wheels are filled with sawdust)

on El Karama, 'small stock' has always been kept as well. However, there have been vicissitudes with the goats and sheep of the ranch. As with the cattle a transformation was wrought upon multi-coloured goats of local, Boer, and Nubian extraction, by white Galla billies from the north of Kenya. Gradually they became a flock of sturdy milk-white, black-skinned beauties. This black skin was immune to sun cancer and the white coat threw off heat – and because they ate every kind of browse the goats did well on El Karama. Angora billies were then introduced to a selected flock of the Gallas, which changed slowly over the years to Angora purebreds. The silver ringlets of their silky coats tumbled in profusion, and

Angora billies

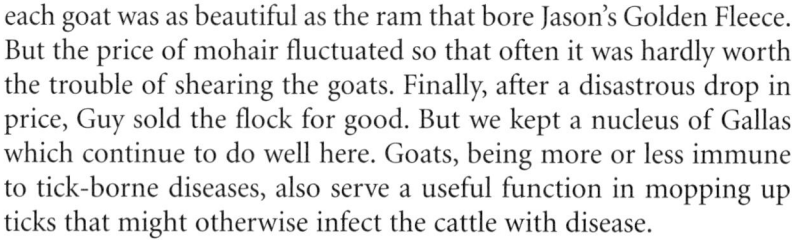

each goat was as beautiful as the ram that bore Jason's Golden Fleece. But the price of mohair fluctuated so that often it was hardly worth the trouble of shearing the goats. Finally, after a disastrous drop in price, Guy sold the flock for good. But we kept a nucleus of Gallas which continue to do well here. Goats, being more or less immune to tick-borne diseases, also serve a useful function in mopping up ticks that might otherwise infect the cattle with disease.

'Kuroo' was a Galla wether goat. He had been given to Elizabeth, daughter of George and Philippa Corse, by Boran people in gratitude, after the Corses had helped a girl who had been badly bitten by a camel. While he was still a kid he had lived in the Corse's Nairobi garden, but it was obvious that it would not be easy to keep

Kuroo

a full-grown goat there unless it were to be tethered for the rest of its life. So Kuroo was given into our care. We drove him home in our Peugeot 404, and many a surprised 'double-take' he elicited from drivers and passengers in other vehicles on the way, as he lay nonchalantly behind the back seat or stood looking out of the rear passenger's windows. Kuroo was a calm and trusting goat, of an enquiring mind, and he seemed to find the journey home with the family interesting and amusing. Outside the Post Office in Nanyuki where we stopped to collect the mail, an admiring group gathered round the car. Even among the goat-familiar people of Kenya where the sight of livestock in cars is not unusual, Kuroo caused a stir. He was beautiful. His coat was short and smooth like snow-white satin; his crescent ears were long and very narrow, grey inside, and turned up at the ends. He had a fine head with a long, straight profile and eyes like clear amber, edged with antimony and pupilled with jet. His black hooves were small and shiny and his short, hairy tail stood erect over his back, showing the line of dark grey skin beneath it.

Kuroo made himself comfortable at home. During the day he was free to come and go as he pleased. At night he slept in a stable, soon climbing into the hay rack which was his bed from then on. Whenever we went out with the dogs for a walk, Kuroo came too. Often he would get left behind as he paused to nibble tempting vegetation, then would canter to catch up, bleating, his neat triangular hooves beating a gritty tattoo on the hard ground. He used this bleat as a contact call rather than to express anxiety. We learnt a lot about what goats like to eat, from Kuroo. He grew quickly and became very strong so that when he decided to devour the yellow daisies growing in a drum by the verandah, no-one could stop him. Sometimes I would find him curled up in the middle of the big double bed, but he was so clean and odourless that it seemed hardly to matter. He was very good-natured but would sometimes butt playfully, and as he was by now taller than the children we were afraid he might hurt them accidentally with his horns. So Kuroo was banished to the ewe boma. He pined and bleated for us for three days and nights, then accepted his lot. But whenever we visited the flock, Kuroo would hurry over to greet us. Each rains, when the kids were born, Kuroo regarded them with a fatherly eye and swaggered about as if he had sired them all himself; for by then the billies had been removed from the flock. So he lived, for many years, a father figure if not a father, to generations of kids. But he always reminded me of an overgrown schoolboy at a sports day, towering over his fellow pupils; for he was by far the tallest goat at the boma.

Dorper sheep, a breed developed from Dorset Horns crossed with Persian Blackheads, were started here in the same way as the cattle and goats; with local animals, including red Maasai fat-tails,

Kids

bred to pedigree Dorper rams. Sheep did well on El Karama and no mutton tasted better, spiced as it was with the small herbs of the bush, than that raised in this lean country. But sheep graze, with quick, small tearing movements, very near to the roots of grasses; and with an increase in wild life and the threat of overgrazing, Dorpers are no longer kept.

Boran bull

Dorper ram

Angora billy

Sahiwal bull

Ranch animals

We were fond of the sheep, which are not, as any good shepherd will tell you, stupid: vulnerable perhaps, and liable to panic because of that vulnerability. The sound of their voices seemed to establish an almost mystical link between the Laikipia bush and the Scottish Highlands, and we miss the sheep.

Soon after we were married, eighty-five breeding ewe-goats were stolen by tribesmen from the north and the herdsman, Abdul, kidnapped. Being a small man, blind in one eye, it was easy for the thieves to hurry him along by the scruff of his great-coat, and he was unable to get away. While Guy alerted the Anti-Stocktheft Unit it was agreed that I should drive northwards to a police post in Mukugodo (a huge tribal area belonging to Maasai and Dorobo people) to warn of the theft and kidnapping, for tracks showed that the goats were travelling in that direction. As it was a long journey over a rough track through wild country I had never been in before, and dark, Mtu' Aburuki (a Meru horseman) came with me to help find the way. When at last we drew up in front of the post, a policeman appeared in the headlights, his machine-gun levelled at us. It took time to persuade him in my newly acquired Swahili that I was a harmless 'Memsahib' on a legitimate errand. By the time we reached home it was morning, and I had had enough of such adventures.

Guy sent some of our men as 'plain-clothes' agents into the Mukugodo and with the help of the Anti Stocktheft Unit nearly all the stolen goats were eventually recovered. Abdul walked home unharmed after his enforced excursion. The place from which he and the goats were abducted has been known as 'Abdul's gully' ever since.

Though selling breeding stock is the mainstay of the ranch we have also to sell steers, cull cows and wether goats for meat. We do not like to see them going away, yet know that they would not have lived at all if people did not eat meat. With factory farms that would be a blessing; but on the ranches, every domestic animal has lived a sun-filled, almost natural life in the freedom of the bush. Vegetables and crops could not be grown in this area commercially instead, but this land will produce an endless supply of good meat if it and its animals, both wild and domestic, are treated with respect and care.

A new venture for the ranch is the breeding of camels to provide milk during the driest weather when we stop milking the cows. Camels show curiosity and will inspect one and one's accoutrements with a thoroughness and interest, and sometimes disapproval, that makes one feel they are very intelligent. They seem to enjoy attention as much as dogs. But to begin with I was nervous of the aristocratic Somali camels. They are huge; much taller than the largest of horses, and I did not know how to interpret their unfamiliar facial expressions. When we were choosing our initial stock a female drifted up noiselessly behind me, startling me and causing me to jump slightly. This fright communicated instantly to the camel which then bucked and stamped across the boma straight for Guy and a cluster of men who were earnestly discussing the merits of another animal.

Sheep boma in evening

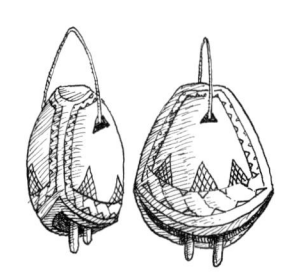

Wooden camel bells

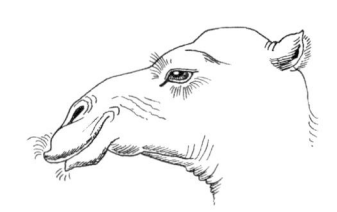

Somali camel

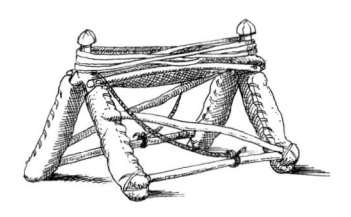

Camel's pack-saddle frame, used with panniers and padded undercloth

THE MEN AND LIVESTOCK 27

They scattered, surprised at this uncharacteristic outburst. I had hidden at once behind the nearest tree, a number of which were growing in the boma, so they never really knew what had caused the disturbance!

Gangling camel foals – strange, woolly children with sea-horse necks, tea-cosy backs and huge eyes fringed with bunches of silky whiskers – are enchanting. It is not surprising that camel herdsmen often seem very fond of their charges. Godana, an ancient Boran who looks after our camels, cried when Guy had to put down one of 'his' camels after it had eaten a poisonous plant.

Sometimes I wonder if the presence of the camels hints at what the future may hold for this beautiful, but fragile and drought-prone land, although in rare years of flood you would not think so: then camels seem out of place. A large number of them are needed to supply a significant amount of milk, although we are breeding the blood of special Pakistani milk camels into our stock. Camels are also rather slow breeders, and the foals delicate when small – so that often it seems we have merely brought in a new set of problems and diseases to cope with.

Godana

Baby camel

Godana

Datura stramonium

Perhaps it is because cattle did not evolve in Africa but travelled slowly southwards with migrating humans over a period of some hundreds of years, that they have not developed immunity to many African diseases as have truly native animals such as eland and zebra. The Maasai, for instance, are said to have arrived in Kenya with their cattle as late as the early eighteenth century. So when buffalo carry corridor disease or East-coast fever, of which they themselves show no serious symptoms, cattle may die quickly unless they are dipped every three days to kill the ticks that carry the disease. (Usually, though, they are dipped every ten days.) At the same time, dipping must weaken the degree of resistance that the cattle of the pastoralists had built up over the years. So the practice of dipping is a mixed blessing, and it seems wrong, to me, to have to depend on poisonous chemicals.

Our cattle do not seem to mind jumping into the dip even though it is out of their depth and they must swim to the far end. As each animal takes a huge leap into the solution which fills a long concrete trench, the boom of the splash is accentuated by the high walls and the corrugated roof above. The pole corridor down which they approach the dip is too narrow to allow more than one to jump at a time; otherwise an animal might fall on top of another and drown it. The dip itself is narrow enough to prevent cattle turning round in it, for it is impossible for them to climb out at the steep end. Very occasionally animals have turned somersaults under water and surfaced facing the wrong way. Once a man bravely jumped in and pulled a bull by its tail to safety, and at other times herdsmen have managed to turn animals by pushing their quarters down and holding their heads up, with poles. As the cows come plodding up from the swirling dip, streaming like water-horses, a number are held for a while in a stone-flagged pen so that the liquid can drain back into the dip. Each month a dip sample is sent away for analysis, and the dip made up to strength again upon the recommendation of the result.

The cattle dip

As there is a second dip on Combretum, cattle can stay on that side of the river indefinitely. Combretum is an ideal nursery for young stock, from weaning at eight months, to about two years of age. Climbing on the rocks strengthens their feet, and they do not get overfat which is an advantage in heifers; for very fat heifers do not get into calf as easily as leaner ones. Mature stock, heavier and

Combretum dip

therefore more likely to damage their legs on the rocks, are kept on the east side of the river, where the land is smooth and rolling.

As is the case with many other ranchers, Guy has nearly always had to be his own veterinary surgeon; for the nearest real vet has often been many hours distance away. All the stock is inoculated; for some diseases only once in a lifetime, for others annually, and sometimes more often: for instance, when there is a foot and mouth challenge, the cattle are inoculated every four months. The inoculation of seven hundred or so cattle in the heat and dust of the yards is quite a job. And there are often individual animals at the homestead for treatment for a variety of ills: sweating-sickness, lumpy-skin, heart-water, anaplasmosis, blackquarter and anthrax are a few of the diseases that may afflict the cattle on the ranch, not to mention broken bones, eye troubles, bruises, lameness and bloat. Occasionally cattle eat poisonous plants, but some of the things that are poisonous to cattle have no effect on eland, and may even be selected by them. Datura stramonium (an alien from South America) is one such plant. Capparis tomentosa, deadly to cattle, camels and people, is also browsed by eland with apparent relish.

Although I quite often act as 'vet' and often as 'veterinary assistant' I am now the only member of the family who cannot administer injections with nonchalant ease. It has always been Guy's sad task to put down animals that are too ill to recover, or to enjoy life anymore.

Because the whole spectrum of wild life occurring naturally in this part of Laikipia is present on the ranch, we occasionally lose an animal to a predator, although the system of bomas, herding, and dogs to give warning reduces this to a minimum. Lions sometimes pick on the cattle, particularly young lions that may not yet be very successful at hunting wild animals. They may cause a stampede through the thorny boma walls by stationing themselves upwind in the dark, and roaring. Then it is easy for the lions to kill a beast in the confusion. Although Guy has shot two lions which were *persistent* cattle-killers since he has been on El Karama, there are often others here that do us no harm, going about their own business of killing their wild prey. 'Simba', Swahili for lion, seems to me a good name for the great cat. There is in its sound a pent fierceness, like the sheathed blade of an assegai; and a fiery tang to it as of wild honey. In spite of the few cattle killed by them, we are glad that there are still lions around to shake the nights of El Karama. A herdsman once told us what a lion is 'saying' when it roars: '*Hii inchi ya nani? Hii inchi ya nani? – Ni yangu! yangu! yangu!*' (Whose country is this? It's mine, mine, mine!) or '*Pokot iko na mikuki mbile, Pokot iko na mkiku mbile; lakini – ni burre! burre! burre!*' (Pokots have two spears, but – it's useless, useless, useless!). Both these phrases in Swahili imitate the first two long roars, followed by short grunts in diminuendo that is the typical roar of a lion, and the words express the kingly arrogance of the sounds perfectly.

Lately we have been housing at night calves, goats or cattle which for some reason or another need to be at the house, in what was previously used as garages – a large, open fronted building in the back yard near the house, divided by inside walls into three 'stables'.

Baby camel
(above and below)

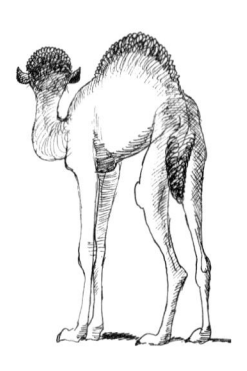

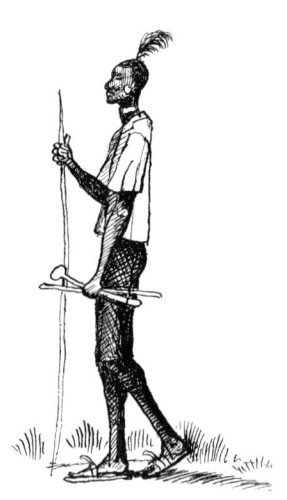

Pokot herdsman

30 ON A KENYA RANCH

Garage stables

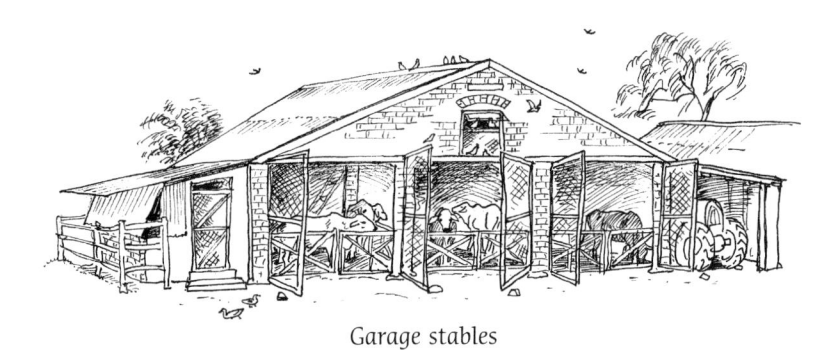

One evening a leopard was seen by the night watchman carrying a goat it had just taken from this building, across the yard. Next evening we built a barricade of hurdles up to the roof in front of each section; but a few nights later the leopard squeezed or climbed in, killing a large calf (ignoring all the others). It ate some of this unfortunate calf inside the building, as it was unable to pull the carcase out. After this, high weldmesh and timber doors were made, which have foiled the leopard. But as a large number of swifts nest and roost in the 'garages' the doors must not be shut until after dark, and have to be opened early each morning.

We are often asked about snakes. Not long ago a large Black-necked spitting-cobra was lying inside the narrow corridor down which cattle were moving during inoculation at the yards. It must have been there for some time when, finally, it could bear the trampling hooves beside it no longer, and came out into the open. It made no attempt to spit or bite. Another time, during the making of a wooden gate, a man bending to pick up a long, heavy stick lying in the grass, found it was a cobra sunning itself, quite unconcerned by the activity nearby. To see a cobra, unaware that it is being watched, pour itself gracefully like a glittering stream through the grass, is a wonderful sight. However we have lost cattle, sheep and goats, two horses, and recently a boma dog (another dog recovered) to snake bite. For the puff-adder, a terrible reptile, is common here.

Elephants can cause problems too. Born to wander the whole vastness of Africa, in Laikipia they are now confined to a much smaller area than in the past, by human settlement. Because of this they have more effect on trees, which may not have a chance to regenerate and grow. It is very expensive to maintain fences where there are elephants and although we have only a few paddocks, the fences are very often broken by them. Sometimes we hear elephants snapping the fences of the paddocks near the house at night, and find poles and posts in the morning like broken spillikins on the ground. Ordinary electric fences will not necessarily keep them out, for elephants can learn how to push them down without getting shocked. We tried for years to grow an eucalyptus plantation in

Leopard tracks (fore and aft)

Black-necked spitting cobra

THE MEN AND LIVESTOCK 31

order to be self-supporting in poles for paddocks and yards, but it was eventually nearly destroyed by elephants in spite of an electric fence. Not that they particularly enjoy eating eucalyptus, but it is the elephants' mission to push down trees. Unless human pressure on the land stops increasing, or elephants learn to leave smallholders alone, the future for them may one day be problematic in Laikipia. At the moment the area holds the largest population of elephants, after Tsavo, in Kenya. Although a number of people and cattle have been killed by them in the district, who could wish them gone, greatest and most wonderful creatures that they are?

Elephants on Amina Ridge

BATS

Silence. Then: tip! tap! tip! tap!
In the roof. Little dark people
Climb over the wire, through a gap,
Then up the ledge to the gable.

The light is just shading
To palest blue – no star yet.
But already it is dusk in the stable
And outside, colour is fading.

Excitement gathers – tip! tap!
Minute figures of sable
Line the ledge thickly – a throng.
They lean as far as they are able.

Suddenly – they're out!
Pouring, silver-winged fountain,
Down, then up! Higher they spout;
Into the sky, over the mountain;
Squeaking delight.

Our Home

Although by some standards our home might be thought rather primitive, one of the happy things to me about it is the way it evolves and the objects in it become part of our lives. New things take a while to fit themselves comfortably into the scheme and to obtain a patina of wear and association. In return for care – polishing or starching, ironing and mending – things give back generously: reassurance, the comfort of familiarity, and memories. An old,

Ranch house with tower

scratched table may take on a rich, deep shine with elbow grease; battered brass door knobs glow like gold when rubbed. The simple concrete floors, in many places cracked, but stained a rich terracotta, seem as fine as marble when polished. Even ugly things that one might not have chosen are known and appreciated for their function and their history. I was surprised when I tried to throw out an ugly steel sugar bowl, at the strength of family resistance to such a move. It had been around ever since they could remember, and they were attached to it: so we use it still. When curtains become old they may be cut up to form part of bright patchwork bed-covers, and later, the bed-covers become rags used in the house for polishing and dusting. This pattern of re-use and relationships seems to apply to almost everything in our home.

Even the rambling house itself evolves, with new rooms added on

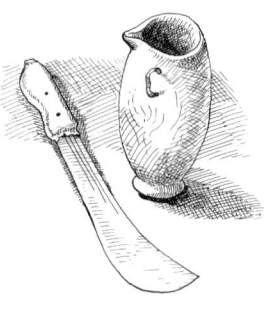

Panga and wooden milk container

here and there in the course of many years. Sometimes the rooms themselves have a changing history. The northern end of our front verandah used to be open; then it was partly enclosed and used as a store. Later it was changed into the school room; a bedroom; and latterly, with improvements, it has become Guy's office. Recently we built a two-storey thatched 'rondavel' on the end of the house – a kind of tower. From there the view is sometimes almost visionary. A herd of impalas may be playing on the slopes of the nearest ridge, their white tails flickering like Morse; while on the crest, families of warthogs feed. There may be a 'woodland' of giraffes in the paddocks and on each successive ridge can be seen groups of zebras. The hind-ends of Grant's gazelles shine like white beacons, while Thomson's gazelles dot the plains. Herds of ox-eyed eland, and oryxes like detachments of lancers, alternate with the cattle. There may be waterbucks, and perhaps even a herd of buffalo which, abandoning their usual caution, have come out to graze in the open before night-fall. And all this may be seen from the house, though not, of course, all at the same time.

Welcome Dover stove

The Three Hills and the Lolldaigas

New windows and new doors are broken through old walls, and because the doors and windows are nearly always open, 'outside' and 'inside' are not clearly defined and many creatures consider the house their home. Fat geckoes behind the pictures, green crickets on the walls, bats in the roof and toads in the drains outside the bathroom and kitchen, swallows in the sitting-room, sleek skinks on the verandah; even the Sugar ants in the cupboards, seem as much lawful denizens as do our staff, our dogs and cats, and we ourselves. I try, however, through cleanliness, to keep cockroaches out of the kitchen! I have grown accustomed to the flat wall spiders which used to fill me with horror (spiders which have remained unchanged for four hundred million years). The number of larger wild creatures we have had actually inside the garden is perhaps surprising, and includes Spotted hyaenas, Side-striped and Silver-backed jackals, Bat-eared fox, White-tailed and Black-tipped mongooses, genets, zorilla, porcupines, African wild cats and leopards, Vervet monkeys and baboons, wart-hogs, Bush duikers, impalas and Bush-babies. If

Porcupine

the orchard is included, then there have also been elephants, bushbucks and giraffes.

Jobs in and around the homestead are still done in the simplest old fashioned way. Firewood is cut with a panga; laborious and time consuming one would have thought. We had a sawing-horse made but the men found sawing an alien and exhausting method and soon abandoned it, returning with relief to the panga.

Bringing in the firewood, with 'coloured' oxen 1972

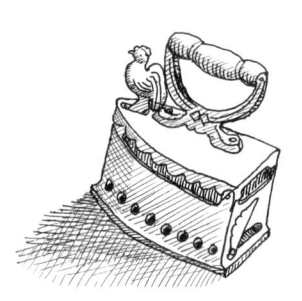

Charcoal iron

Water for baths was heated, until recently, in a forty-four gallon drum over an open fire in the evenings (a Tanganika boiler), now replaced by an improved version which uses much less firewood, and stores the heated water in an insulated tank from where it is piped to the house. Laundry is washed by hand with cakes of laundry soap in a tub outside, and hung to dry in the fresh air. For pressing the laundry we use an iron, made in India, which is filled with red-hot embers from the stove. It has an unnerving habit of opening unexpectedly and spilling its contents, so many of our clothes have small holes burnt in them. When I was still struggling with Swahili I asked the cook, who was attending at a dinner party, for another spoon (or so I thought). He looked a little startled and was gone a surprisingly long time. When he returned to the dining room he announced the iron was now ready. Perhaps he felt that, if I was eccentric enough to start ironing in the middle of dinner, he had better humour me.

Cooking is done on a cast iron Dover stove, so that the kitchen walls are darkened with wood smoke, though they are scrubbed and whitewashed once a year. Pots and pans are scoured clean with ashes and water because the open drain from the kitchen leads to fruit trees, which would be damaged by detergents. I brought a silver tea pot to Kenya when we were married but sent it back almost at once, after it had been enthusiastically scrubbed with wire wool. It seemed out of place. Food-blenders, hair-driers, washing machines, television and computers have yet to find their way here, as our generator is used only for electric light in the evenings.

Drinking water is taken from tanks in which rain from the rooves

Hot water system (Tanganika boiler)

is collected, and is boiled before use. Two churns of this cool water ready for drinking or other purposes, are kept in the kitchen.

The garden used to be a long rectangle hemmed in by a low brick wall which separated it from the paddock and orchard in front of the house, and seemed to keep the bush at bay. Guy had no time to think about a garden, and it had reverted to rough grass, with a few succulents along the front of the house and by the wall, which had been planted by his mother. The wall itself had begun to lean outwards and was propped with old grey fence-posts. On giving one of these posts a shove one day, the wall moved a little. I had an exciting idea to which Guy agreed absent-mindedly while sitting over papers at his desk. Returning to the wall and removing all the posts, I gave it a hard push. The whole thing fell with a muffled thump! In no time the other side was down too! It was as if a giant, compelled to hold his breath for years, had at last expanded his chest in a great sigh of relief; for the garden was now free to spread itself to the orchard gate. On each side was the bush, stretching away to the Lolldaiga hills on one side and to Mt. Kenya and the Aberdares on the other.

In the dry weather the grass of the lawn turns Naples yellow, and is burnt away by the sun to prickly, nubbly roots in the dust, and the light, reflected from the oven-hot ground, is thrown in at the windows so that one has to turn away or screw up one's eyes. But during the rains the green grass is often long, and covered with star heads from which pollen bursts in little clouds when disturbed by bees which come to pack their leg-baskets with it. Then the grass is cut with slashers and for a day or two is left to lie, turning almost blue as it dries in the sun. We rake up this sweet hay and store it for the rabbits, Gunia Gasson, Theophilus Warren and Raggylugs, the last of a line of small animals kept by the children when they were younger. Their hutches and runs are under the jacarandas which are sometimes smothered with bunches of mauve bell flowers; and the grass underneath the trees is covered with a lilac-blue carpet. A muted roar can be heard in the mornings as thousands of bees gather nectar in the canopy, while others drone over the carpet below, confused by the scent and colour of the fallen flowers. When the jacarandas flower, the climbing bougainvillea that blankets some of the largest trees in the garden with a hanging mass of brick pink and crimson, is also in full flower.

Once year we decided to leave the lawn uncut until we had a heavy crop of hay. It was odd to be surrounded by an almost waist-high jungle of grass which pressed close around the house and gave it a derelict and secretive air. A neighbour, after a beer or two on the verandah, confessed to being 'bamboozled' by it and unable to find his way out at the gate. But the long grass provided a good supply of

Speckled Mouse birds

Theophilus Warren

Pawpaw tree

caterpillars for the feeding of various fledglings I was trying to raise at the time.

The orchard is a narrow acre beyond the garden. Because it is watered and manured it is an oasis. Clumps of banana trees rustle their leathery leaves with a sound like falling rain; nostalgic in dry weather. They bear stems of small, sweet bananas subtended by strange purple flowers. There are paw-paw trees topped with tufts of palmate leaves under which cluster breast-shaped fruit. Crimson-cheeked mangoes hang in heavy bunches on their dark-foliaged trees, while green and shiny avocadoes dangle from overhead branches. Before the rains, blossom bursts on the peach trees, but we never have enough of the peaches as the birds eat nearly all of them. There are oranges, sweet for eating, bitter Seville for marmalade; tangerines and grapefruit. The air is often scented with lemon blossom and by the intricate flowers of pomme-d'ors. Here and there are the pre-historic, knobbed fruit of Custard apples, sweet and white inside but full of black pips. Loquats and Cherry guavas are coming into bearing at the bottom of the orchard.

Each morning for an hour or two, water runs sparkling in shallow furrows under the trees and between clumps of Himalayan blackberries. When the children were small they loved to float the canoe-shaped pods of Flame trees on these furrows, and to make little water wheels of leaves and sticks.

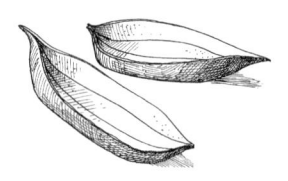

After a bad drought in 1984 we ploughed a strip beside the orchard and planted it with lucerne for the horses and Bonar grass for making silage. Bonar grass-cutting parties are an occasion for laughter and chatter among the men involved, and the cheerful sounds float up to the house, punctuated by the rhythmical swish of the hand-turned cutter. The chopped grass is buried in small pits, like a line of graves. If the rains fail or are delayed, this silage is dug up and mixed with other feed for the cattle. Upon going down to the mares' stable one morning, I saw six men pressing the silage down in one of these pits. They were going slowly round and round, close together, stamping in unison as if dancing – indeed, they were dancing – and all their teeth shone white as they smiled.

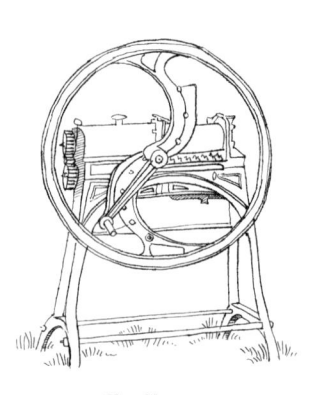

Elephants have broken into the orchard, and jackals and Vervet monkeys, mouse-birds and bulbuls are attracted to the fruit. In dry weather bushbucks occasionally come from the river to eat the lucerne, and duikers squeeze under the gate. If the orchard is left unguarded during the day baboons may raid it, as it is easy for them to climb over the kei-apple hedge. They post watchmen up strategic thorn trees to keep an eye on the gardener, and often enter during rain when he or she has run for shelter. And sometimes blights and scales affect the fruit trees. But in spite of all this, the orchard produces abundantly enough. A variety of insects keep each other in check, and blights run their course and disappear without the use of poisons and pesticides on our part. The only remedy used is an occasional spraying with soapy water or sprinkling with wood-ash; the only fertilisers are manure, ash, and rotting vegetation which are mixed together to make compost.

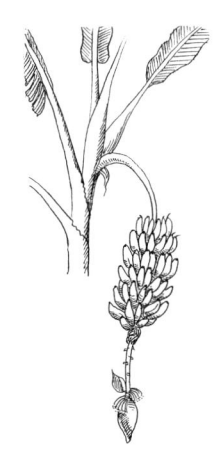

From time to time there have been elegant gardeners in the orchard; notably Ruge, a beautiful Boran, wife of Gumbi, our senior horseman at the present time. And there was Asha, a tiny bird-like old woman, half Boran, half Kikuyu, who once somehow set fire to her clothes while lighting her paraffin lamp in the evening. Wonderfully brave and stoical, she spent many months in hospital and was afterwards partly disabled. Abdia, a young wife who had never gardened before, was so excited over her first seedlings that she cried when the birds ate them.

The 'farmyard' is an open area of grazed grassland behind the house and garden where, over many years, a number of buildings have grown up. The ranch artisan or 'fundi', and his assistant and general workers, do the building with local materials, so the houses look as if they have grown in their places. There is nothing harsh or alien about even the newest of them except for the corrugated-iron on some of the rooves. Other rooves are thatched with makuti (coconut palm leaves) from the coast, or papyrus from the Rumuruti swamp not far to the west. Under many of these rooves live large colonies of bats, which issue, silver-winged, from the eaves each evening, like living fountains.

Bananas and flower

The stables

The 'fundi' has his open-air workshop near the stables, under an acacia tree. There the ground is covered with ringlet shavings of pink cedar, yellow pine and white cypress. And some way behind on slightly higher ground are the long, whitewashed buildings of the labour lines.

The posho store is one of the original Italian brick buildings, a stone-floored room aisled inside with heavy wooden benches worn smooth and polished with use. On these are stacked sacks of horse and poultry feeds, and of maize flour and sugar for the employees of

Posho store

Soap, tea and sugar

Stallion's stable

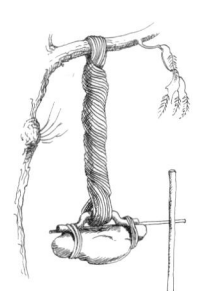

Twisting riems

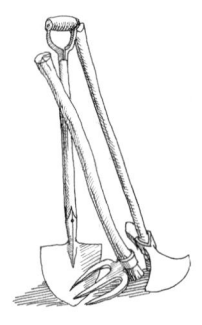

Spade and jembes

the ranch and their families. A mealy fragrance pervades the air as you step down into the twilight of the interior, and you at once feel content and at peace, though why this should be I do not know. By the doorstep hop tiny Red-billed fire finches, glowing like live coals; and the murmured and clucked conversations of gleaning hens are sleepy-sounding in the sunlight.

Once a week everyone on the ranch comes to this store for supplies: packets of tea, long bars of pungent yellow soap, matches, measures of meal, and coarse sugar, and sometimes fruit or vegetables from the orchard. Fat or ghee is available in dry weather, and beans and powdered milk. There are cheap, brown blankets edged with stripes of ochre, blue or red, and shiny new metal karais. But the store is not the only source of supplies for ranch employees, because the weekly vehicle going to town to collect fuel, feeds and hardware, takes those who wish to shop. At the back of the store stands the old scales upon which sacks are weighed, and assorted family jetsam waits in the rafters for when it may be taken down, dusted and used again.

Some way from the posho store, past the brick stable for the stallion, is an old maize-crib, built by the Osbornes, that has walls of wooden slats so that sunlight enters it in dazzling horizontal stripes. It is raised off the ground on rows of cedar posts, and one climbs in via a square hatch at one end. The crib has not held maize for forty years but is used instead for the storage and drying of skins. Along the floor the fresh skins are laid out flat, each covered with dairy salt. On the walls and from the roof are suspended and stretched other skins, chestnut of impala, white of goat, warm brown of the big cattle skins. Others, already salt-cured and dried, are folded in square packages at the far end of the crib and numbered with leather tags. Strips of eland or waterbuck hide, oiled with tallow, hang from a branch of an old pepper tree nearby, a heavy rock suspended from them which is turned periodically to twist and stretch the strips. These will be 'riems' for use with the ox-carts. They do not chafe through as rope does, and are very strong. The cutting of riems is an art, for where a skin is thick the strip must be cut narrow, and where it is thin, wider; so that after stretching the riem will be of even width. They are cut in a spiral from the outside of the skin inwards, to obtain length.

Near the skin store are the ranch clerk's offices, two wood-lined rooms in which the ranch books are entered up and the diary and horse patrol reports are written each evening by lamplight. Cattle record-cards are kept there in long, narrow boxes. Rosettes won at past shows hang in festive but faded lines, while jembes and pangas lean in the corners. Beyond these rooms the roof projects to form a shady porch where Little swifts have plastered their nests thickly. All

Maize-crib skin-store

*Mixing salt for the cattle. Back yard El Karama. July '99.
(Jaspa intimidating Nyuki).*

Mixing cattle salt

View from heifer boma looking west towards Combretum

Looking N.E. Combretum house. Dec '95.

House at Combretum

Some Sahiwal Cows
from sketches

Sketches of Sahiwal cows

Giraffes on Airstrip Ridge

Sahiwal cows from Nyamuluki Hill

Ratel with hive and honey guide

Patrol — Gumbi Huko Dawa (Boran) riding Alfarata.

On Patrol

Boran cattle at dawn

Mt. Kenya from Itiama's hill. Early morning, August '99

day parties of foraging swifts spiral and whirl high above the farmyard, and when they sweep in to roost, the air is filled with their metallic trills.

The stables, seen from the office porch, are used not only by horses but by Ethiopian swallows which nest there in numbers. The old roof of wooden shingles was left in place under the newer iron, and on these shingles the swallows build their cup-shaped nests. Striped swallows, however, prefer to plaster their flask-nests in the garage.

In the new power house squats a generator. But for twelve years we did not have electricity, relying on pressure lamps, and latterly on hurricane lamps. Pressure lamps gave a better light but were hot and noisy, with a habit of bursting into flames if one forgot to keep them well pumped. Hurricane lamps seemed preferable because, being

Striped swallow's nest

Cold room and power house

silent, the sounds of the bush could be heard coming through the open windows – as they still can. From dusk, the insect orchestra is so constant and familiar that one has to make a conscious effort to register it, except when Burrowing crickets make their ear-numbing buzz – powerful as road drills when heard nearby – which seems to resonate right inside one's head. There is always the yapping of zebras, and the growling and snorting of an impala ram herding females in the paddock in front of the house. Now and again a leopard 'saws' and is answered by a clamour of barks from roosting baboons at the river. Sometimes Verreaux eagle-owls perch on the highest garden jacaranda and make a duet of ultra-deep hoots followed by a hollow rumbling that I can only describe as 'plank-dropping', while a lion's distant roar is like a repeated shudder in the air. The protesting squeals of horses from their night-paddock behind the house, the barking of our dogs, the trumpeting of elephants, muted voices from the ayah's house in the garden; all are familiar sounds of the night,to us. The following nightwatchmen's reports for a single night around headquarters are quite typical of those we receive each morning:

A Burrowing cricket

Verreaux Eagle owl

OUR HOME 41

Impala ram chasing off youngster

MUNGATHIA (watchman 1)
11 pm.   Leopard at pump paddock.
12.30   Leopard at Taxiway.
1 am   Elephants at Nyumbani Luggah.

MAHUINJI (watchman 2)
9 pm   Leopard at Nyumbani Luggah.
3 am   Elephants at Dam ya Nyumbani.
4 am   A Lion roared at Segera – pump-side.

MUNYATTA (watchman 3)
11 pm   Buffaloes at Outside Cottage Paddock.
3–4 am   Leopard at pump paddock.

The house reminds me of a ship hove-to in the sea of the bush and the other buildings are part of a fleet. In the evenings the gold of the lights and the red of the hot-water fires beckon welcomingly, as from portholes. The horizons at night are as dark and mysterious as the sea, the distances as blue in the day; and the land of El Karama is like slow swells rolling across the ocean of Laikipia.

Evening 'screaming party' of Little swifts

CHANGES

Man's changes steal on the land.
Rich woodland, same for a million years,
Fades like sleight of hand -
Bare ground,
Fields of tares,
And dirty town.
Seed birds shoaling pristine air,
Now poisoned - shocking!
Knocked down in flight;
No more flocking.
Woods are charcoal cooking fires.
Consuming blight
Spread by human mind and hand,
Steals changes on the land.

The Town

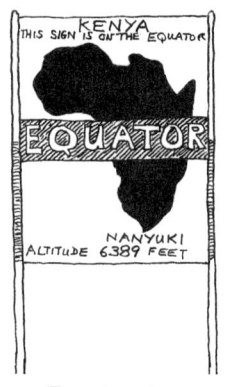

Nanyuki, our home town, is on the Equator, which is marked by a sign showing exactly where this runs. Around the sign a craft market has sprung up. So profitable is this market that another 'Equator' was set up some hundreds of yards farther along the road, and the market there is just as profitable! Although the town appears quite small as you drive through on the road from Nairobi to Isiolo, it has a large population, and the little huts and houses of the settlers on its outskirts seem to spread farther into the country each month. There is also a large 'majengo' or slum area where the small, single-storey houses are of timber and mud with rust-brown rooves of flattened iron containers laid on like shingles. The rooves have an oriental cast, slanting out over narrow verandahs in front, held up by painted wooden posts. The earthen streets are arranged, to some early plan, in straight lines leading from each other at right angles, and some of them are of generous width and lined with trees, so that in spite of the poverty and dirt synonymous with slums everywhere, this part of Nanyuki has a certain picturesque appeal nevertheless.

Our vehicle, approaching town from the west, passes many new dirt lanes flanked by rows of small, concrete houses. At the end of each litter-speckled alley could be seen, for a while, the clean open bushland of whistling-thorn and red-oat grass from which the town

Equator sign

Nanyuki club

has sprung. Each tiny house has, somehow unexpectedly, its television aerial, and each little compound is decorated with bright laundry hung out to dry: mauve and yellow sheets printed with gaudy flowers, chequered cloths of red and white, and crocheted table-cloths and shawls in fluorescent pink and lime-green. Along the edge of the road, improvised stalls display small pyramids of tomatoes, bananas and avocados. In the evening, women fan braziers upon which nutty maize-cobs are roasted for sale to hungry passers-by. We pass a little white mosque, toy-like with blue cut-out minarets, cushioned in dark trees and enclosed by a wall stained along the bottom by the orange earth (Nanyuki means 'red', in Maasai). There are crowds of people. On Sundays the throng is dressed in its brightest clothes as it enters or leaves the churches of many denominations that are to be found in the town – Anglican and Catholic, Pentecostal and Presbyterian, Baptist, Quaker and 7th Day Adventist. Bicycles groan under the weight of sewn-together, double-length sacks of charcoal brought in from the country; or with passengers sitting over the back wheels, their legs stuck out to the sides for balance. The end of the street appears to be blocked by Mount Kenya, towering over the Pride of Bolivia trees, and over the nefarious ramifications of the town; its peaks pristine with snow and seemingly near enough to be touched. At other times you would not guess the mountain was there, behind a certain bright opacity of the air.

In 1942 Guy's mother set up and ran a tea room in Nanyuki for the soldiers fighting in the Ethiopian campaign. The first strip of tarmac the town could boast was laid in front of this house, to prevent the dust which billowed in whenever convoys of army lorries passed through on their way to the Northern Frontier District. Now the centre of town has parallel tarmac streets on either side of the main road, the verges of which are planted with bougainvillea, scarlet and pink poinsettias, jacarandas, gum trees, exotic pines and deep-shaded 'bombax' trees. The main street is lined with false-fronted 'dukas' (shops) and raised pavements, which give Nanyuki rather the look of a town in the Old West of America. This impression was heightened for a time when there was a fashion, among the jaunty-stepping young men, in worn-over high-heeled cowboy boots, relics of a past vogue in other lands. There is a clock tower whose clock (before the tower was taken over as an advertisement by a well known firm) was stuck for some years at 10.30. Small boys sometimes herd goats on the town verges or leave them to their own devices as they, themselves, scamper admiringly and importunately alongside visiting British soldiers: for each year battalions from different regiments are billeted in the show ground near the Sports Club.

A cafe, well known meeting place, is called the Marina; though

The Mosque

Chorisia speciosa

Our landcruiser

the town is uncompromisingly land-locked. Another reference to non-existent sea-side is a sign pointing to the 'Silent Sea Dry Cleaner and Hotel', though perhaps this 'sea' could be considered an interpretation of the horizon of the Laikipia plateau, which can be seen stretching flat and blue to the west. The 'Day and Night Club' promises lively goings-on belied by the generally sleepy atmosphere of the main street.

When El Karama employees are in town they eat at the Arab's 'City Butchery and Best Tea Room' where they also stay overnight if necessary. The City Butchery is a meeting place for people of many tribes, and Maasai, Samburu, and Turkana are to be seen outside it, in red or black 'shukas', the Samburu women with flat, wide necklaces of beads and tin, their shaven heads shining with ochre. Graceful Somali and Boran women in flowing garments, and their lean and hawk-faced men with shawls about their heads and shoulders, spice the drab surroundings with brilliant colour. Kikuyu 'mamas' pass, stout-bodied, laden 'kiondos' suspended from brow-straps on their backs, pangas in hand. They wear an ubiquitous uniform of knee-length dress, knitted cardigan and back-knotted headcloth, as they move to or from maize and bean patches outside the town, their wrinkled feet plopping tiredly in the dust. Younger women carry babies bound with cloths to their backs and neatly covered with clean towels. Umbrellas spread to shade the babies from the sun used always to be black, but now that multi-coloured ones are available from China, they are all the rage. A number of old men, well known characters, hobble to stare through car windows with turtle-lidded eyes, hoping for alms.

At the matatu rank opposite the city Butchery, 'matatus' (taxis) hoot and tout for 'fares'. Many are decorated, some with gazelles pursued by ravening lions, and each has a name painted over the back door – 'The G. Samaritan', 'Jasho Tours' (Sweaty tours), and 'Private Dinosaur'. Buses with names like 'Land Missile' and 'Buffalo Soldier' vie with each other for custom. Even the lorries that lumber and snort into town under incubi of diesel fumes, have names: 'Sauti ya Ndovu' (Voice of the Elephant), 'Trust in God' and 'Inshallah'. Carts pulled by dispirited donkeys creak, over-laden, along the pitted roads; and nowadays herds of bewildered camels are sometimes seen moving along the main street on the long walk to Nairobi, to be slaughtered for the growing population of Somalis there.

One of the sad things about Africa, though perhaps it applies to all countries to a lesser or greater degree, is the callous treatment of animals by many (but by no means all). The sight of starveling donkeys, sometimes with raw wounds, staggering under loads far too great for them and with unsuitable 'harness' which puts all the weight of a cart upon their necks, often being made to trot or even

Kikuyu mama

A Matatu

canter by being beaten from the top of the load by people too lazy to walk themselves, must distress anyone who travels the roads of the country. Yet who knows what hardening effect poverty, and a daily struggle for existence, might have upon one's attitude to animals? It is not, however, always the poorest that are so thoughtless about the animals they are lucky enough to possess.

One day I noticed a beggar sitting under a shop window on the pavement. He was bent, although still young, and blind – a small and puny Somali. A polythene bag came blowing along the pavement on an eddy of dust and brought up against his feet. Feeling inside and finding it empty, he cast it off to go scraping away again in the wind. After a while he took a spotless cloth from inside his jacket, laid it on the pavement and kneeling on it, bowed his head so that his forehead touched the cloth. It was an act of humility and dignity, quite without self-conscious ostentation, and I felt somehow rebuked for having pitied him. He was living a life of self-denial and extreme discomfort that he had not chosen but which he apparently accepted without bitterness, and each day he gave praise to Allah. Authorities had wanted to move this beggar away though he had no other means of making a living, but the owner of the shop outside which he sat, told them that he liked having him there; that he was a good example to the rest of us.

In the busy town markets, alleys between stalls are shaded with billowing walls of khangas (cloths worn by women and printed in bright colours and bold designs), striped kikois, and the red and pink togas favoured by Maasai and Samburu. Plastic buckets and basins are ranged in multi-coloured tiers next to lines of 'thousand-milers' (sandals made of tyre treads and inner tube), cheap looking-glasses and bright aluminium sufurias (cooking pots). Hanging outside some of the booths are giant imitation packets of tobacco made from banana fibre to indicate that tobacco is sold inside; or bunches of leafy twigs where 'Miraa', a chewable narcotic tree shoot, is obtainable. The many bars of town throb with the cheerful, rhythmic music of Kenya, rendered tinny by over-amplification on cheap radios.

Fruit stall

Khanga

Pretty house

THE TOWN

Orders for hardware for the ranch are filled at the 'Modern Sanitary Store', for stationery at the 'United Store', and groceries from the 'Settler's Store'. Our mail is collected once a week from a locked box in a wall of such boxes at the blue-painted post office. From a yellow kiosk in front of the post office brisk business is done selling sweets one at a time, and tickets for the National Charity Sweepstake. Maize for our ranch employees is ground monthly at a mill in a back street undulating with ruts and corrugations, where everything and everyone is covered with a heavy coating of white meal. And all official business is carried out in a special compound of wooden government offices, demarcated by lines of white-washed stones, shaded by weeping Eucalyptus and ancient pepper trees, which was, for a time, surrounded by a graveyard of abandoned government vehicles.

At the Sports Club, before I came, there used to be horse racing. It was there that Guy and I first met, when a polo tournament was in progress. For years there was polo at the club and Guy used to play, having walked his horses from the ranch. One of his best polo ponies, Mistral, a tall flea-bitten grey gelding, was an ex-army pack horse bought for the equivalent of £5. But the polo ground is now a golf course. The old grandstand which remained until recently, and the sway-backed lines of wooden stables, have gone.

The Nanyuki river runs through the town, usually clear, and very cold from the snows of the mountain. Along its banks grow cedar and Syzigium trees and mossy podos upon whose branches delicate epiphytic orchids cling. The purring cries of turacos, the trumpeting of hornbills and shrill whistles of Red-fronted parrots echo amongst them, and at night the shrieks of Tree hyraxes mingle with the barking of dogs to serenade town residents. The river runs parallel to 'Lunatic Lane' (now Simba Lane) – which was a residential road in early Colonial days, as it is still – on its way to lower altitudes where it joins the Uaso Nyiro just north, and downstream, of El Karama.

A day in town is usually exhausting, the chores seldom finished before dark. Then, it is a relief to leave the noise and the dust, the crowds and the evidence of poverty, to pass under the pole at the check point at the end of the last stretch of pot-holed tarmac outside town, and to set off on the murram road which heads into the wide, free darkness of the land (just as a ship leaves the pierheads of a harbour for the open sea). With every mile the tensions of the town drop away to be replaced slowly, the farther one goes, with the quiet and positive peace of the bush.

EARLY CHILDHOOD

A time for slow walks with many stops
To look at flowers - an ant,
And a grasshopper's hops;
Contented conversation and childish games
In endless, drowsy afternoons.
It was happy, early childhood -
An immortal, timeless time
Unshaded by any future; no past -
Suspended always in bright day;
With no knowledge that it would not last.

The Children

There was perhaps no happier time for me than that between the birth of our children and their having to go away to school. Of course there was worry when they were ill, as we were so far from our doctor in Nairobi. But we had a telephone then and we would consult the doctor on that. It was the kind you wind the handle of to call Exchange, on a party line with thirteen others, each of whom had their own code of 'longs and shorts'. But often it did not work when it was needed and eventually we had it taken away, though the eight miles of poles which carried the wires from the road still stood until recently. When I first came, the telephone had not yet been put in, and we used to ride on horses five miles to the nearest telephone which was housed, mysteriously, in a small shack in the bush on the ranch to the south of us. I remember trotting home in moonlight after making such a call, and the exhilaration of the ride as Mistral shied at black and silver shadows cast across the track by trees. Guy had managed to speak to me occasionally, in Scotland, before we were married, from this primitive telephone. It no longer exists. We now rely on a radio to get messages to and from the 'outside'.

Both our daughters were born in Nairobi; but our son, Murray, in Nanyuki, in the (then) tiny Cottage Hospital, because he arrived unexpectedly ten days early. When I was waiting for our first daughter to be born, tired and frustrated because it took so long, Guy was advised to take me for a drive to try to hurry matters. He was horrified at the idea. We set off from the hospital along the Mombasa

The old telephone (from memory)

E.A.R. engine

road which runs near the Nairobi National Park fence, parallel to the railway. Every time I had a contraction Guy stopped, so we progressed in nervous fits and starts to the puzzlement of other drivers. We saw two steam engines and, eventually, a rhinoceros just inside the Park fence. He was snorting clouds of vapour from his nostrils and curling his tail over his back as he walked. Maybe these excitements helped, for Laria arrived not too long after we returned to the hospital.

For some days we could not decide what to call our baby in spite of having thought of many possible and impossible names before she was born. One afternoon Guy visited, looking determined. 'She is to be called Laria' he announced. He had consulted with the men on the ranch and they had suggested 'Laria', being the name given by the Meru for a place on El Karama which holds water and green grass long after the rest of the ranch has dried up in the rainless season.

One of the lovely things about being with the children when they were a little bigger (as it is with all children, of course), was hearing the things they said, the conversations they held. I wrote down some of these and wish now that I had done so more often. When Laria was three she asked 'Do the stars walk with the moon, do they?' She had noticed the moon moved across the sky and wondered if the stars did too, but I thought at the time it was just a poetic fancy of hers, not what it was: scientific interest. But Laria was also poetic, for she said 'The moon is the moth's sun'. At four years old she came to me once, very excited – 'When I was at the kukus (chickens) I saw a little brown thing running, running *very* fast on its tip toes. And it looked at me with its little brown, and little tinkling eyes. And it was a *mouse*!' When she was six she informed me that the ground was 'horrified with siafu' (safari ants), and another time, of vultures. 'There are millions of eagles – like scales in the sky'.

Murray, nearly four, when asked if he would like to go to the seaside again, answered 'Mmmm – is there still a big lake there?'. And, 'When I grow up, I will run out at night'. 'What will you see, Murray, if you run out at night?'. 'I might see the shadows of the hyaenas', he answered, his eyes very round. And 'I am going to hunt all the poachers who kill animals', 'When you grow up, Murray?' – 'No, after tea'. Laria asked Murray how he could bear to eat so much sugar, and he responded indignantly 'Bears *like* sugar!'. Just before going to sleep one evening he said drowsily 'I hate mosquitoes, but I love dung beetles'. When the girls informed him that our stallion, Karama, was half Arab, he said he knew – 'His front half is Arab'.

I heard this conversation between Bella, then six, and her cousin Andrew, aged four, when they were supposed to be asleep – Bella:

White-bellied mouse

Dung beetle

'Anou, as far North as you can possibly go, far away in the North – miles and *miles* to the North – millions and millions, and billions and billions, and fillions, and trillions' (I wondered when she would stop) 'of miles to the North, it is very, *very* cold, Anou, and it's *always* dark, and there is snow – nine times as deep as this house, Anou. As this *house*! And there is nothing to eat'. Thoughtful pause, then Andrew, matter of factly – 'You could eat carrots'. Bella, surprised: 'Carrots? You couldn't eat carrots all the time!'. 'Why not?' 'Well, think of eating nothing but carrots every, every day. Nothing but carrots all the time. It would be horrible. And besides, Anou, you couldn't grow them there. *Nothing* grows in the snow, Anou'.

There were always questions, such as 'Are our legs our back arms?' or 'Mummy, what's the very farthest away on all the Ball? Is it Noah's Arctica?' And I loved the strange words they often invented for things before they had quite grasped the right ones: 'pezoon' for pencil, 'capeela' for caterpillar, 'ponbeel' for hornbill, and 'tetterbeck' (waterbuck). The 'Three-fourbla tree', a large Candelabra euphorbia, was used as a landmark and goal on walks when the children were little. Once they began to write, we were often amused by their unconventional spelling – as when Murray captioned his drawing of a very large snake 'Woot pithoon' (wood python).

As is customary in Kenya we had an Ayah (nanny) to help when the children were small, so they grew up speaking both English and Swahili and often a mixture of the two. The evening we took on stout Esther Chipkimboi as Ayah ('The very best Ayah I have *never* known' according to Laria then), I was giving Murray his bath in the basin. 'I will do that' she announced authoritatively in Swahili (for she speaks little English), 'You go and give the girls their supper'. I went obediently and have been obeying her ever since. Esther's eyes are an unusual pale amber colour – perhaps inherited from her Ethiopian father. She takes command of situations, and now that the children are grown up, she is Empress of the kitchen. She has taught us many things while she has lived with us, such as how to sew sheep skins and goat skins into rugs so that the seams will not tear, and how to make thread for the sewing out of the sheath of the back muscles of larger animals, such as cattle and eland. When this sheath is dried it can be split into long fibres which, rolled together, make fine, strong thread; also good for sewing beads onto leather. On walks in the bush Esther showed us plants from which glue can be made for fledging arrows; and which berries and toadstools are safe for eating and those that are poisonous. We learnt how to make a refreshing tea from the inner bark of Rhus natalensis (particularly strengthening after childbirth, she assured me). From the inner bark of Acacia gerrardii, she made almost unbreakable string and rope. She told us tales of her girlhood, when her mother's people, the

To the Threefourbla tree

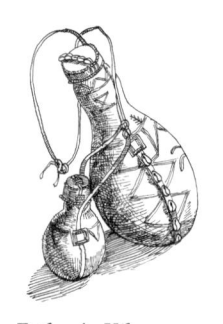

Esther's Kibuyus

Nandi, preferred to live with plenty of space around them, each family homestead widely separated from its neighbour and each hidden in its grove of woods. Esther cannot swim but she remembers how, when out herding her family's cattle, she would cross a river holding onto the tail of a cow and thus come safely to the other side. Sometimes she and others would climb a high hill in Nandi-land from which they could see Mt. Kenya, far away. If there was new snow on its shoulders it was time to plant – for rain was imminent.

The mountain with new snow

For birthdays and Christmas Esther has always made presents for the children: bracelets of cowrie shells braided onto rawhide, beaded belts, honey-coloured gourds decorated with burnt patterns, capped with minutely-beaded leather and smoked inside with burning mukinyea twigs to give milk a delicious flavour; or toy huts of woven fibre thatched with red-oat grass, and clay cattle and sheep in cardboard and lichen bomas. For me, and my mother in Scotland, she plaited table mats of banana fibre from the orchard and tiny, tightly woven baskets of grass stems.

Toy house

There were also the rest of the household staff so that, in a way, our family has had its African members. One of the many advantages of not having to do the cooking and much of the housework myself was that there was time to be with the children. Even shopping is usually done with the aid of lists sent to town with the weekly ranch vehicle, though this method sometimes produces unexpected results; as when I ordered ten cakes of soap and received ten little cakes each with a glace cherry on top – and only one piece of soap. But such quaint uncertainties are characteristic of life on El Karama. There was the time we were apprised of the imminent arrival of some well known politician, who was to take a short cut through the ranch with his entourage, and who expected to be given lunch by us on his way. There would not be more than fifteen people, we were told. But to my astonishment Esther cooked nearly a whole sack of potatoes and a mountain of meat. She knew what she was about. Cars began to arrive in the back yard at about 4.30 in the afternoon – more and more of them; and people filled the house and garden. In the end there were sixty five guests, and all

Banana fibre mat

THE CHILDREN 53

were somehow fed. Why there were so many, where they had all come from, and where they were going we never discovered. It was a shy housewife's nightmare fulfilled.

on Esther's back

It did not seem long before the children were old enough to start formal education. As it was too far to Nanyuki for them to go to day school there, I taught the three of them from the age of four until they were eight and a half, eight, and seven years old, with Mrs. Graham's postal primary courses sent from the coast, and marked by her each week. This was not altogether easy as I had no formal experience as a teacher, and we were sometimes strongly tempted to miss lessons. The children found it hard to concentrate at times during less popular subjects, as we worked on the verandah from which we could see giraffes coming to drink at a trough just outside the garden. Butterflies visited the flowers along the front of the verandah, birds were free and singing in the garden trees, and there were so many other absorbing occupations waiting for when lessons should be over. But on the whole lessons were a happy and constructive period, and the children did well.

Animals, of course, have always been basic and vital to El Karama. Murray, when hardly taller than a kid himself, used to help Laria herd the 'hospital' goats which were kept at headquarters for treatment. They took them into the top of the river paddock to browse. Laria and Bella helped to dose the sheep and goats when they came

Herding the hospital goats

Children with goats Murray and Laria

to the back yard. It was exciting to see the solid, moving mass of animals on a forest of twinkling legs, their hooves sounding like heavy rain on the hard ground. The children would put the sheep through the blue-green copper sulphate foot bath; and they watched when the sheep and goats were weighed. One day I heard grunts coming from their room and found Laria and Bella struggling to hang Murray up by a cloth round his middle to a hook on the wall. He was being a goat and they were weighing him.

Guy taught all the children to shoot with an air rifle, Murray being the keenest. For his first lesson he carried a cardboard carton with a target painted on it to the Front Paddock. The carton was nearly as big as himself so that only his thin legs showed beneath it. After it was set up some yards away, Guy shot at, and hit, the bull's eye as his demonstration. When it was Murray's turn he sat so long that we could sense, through the dusk, the barrel wavering with effort. Finally a shot was loosed. 'I got it!' he exclaimed. 'You didn't get the bull's eye, Murray?' asked Laria, full of admiration. 'No – the box!' he answered proudly. He became a good shot and now keeps everyone on the ranch supplied with meat, when he is at home. However, at the age of three, he had been taken to the meat-house where an impala was being skinned and cut up. I had mistakenly shielded him from this sight so it was finally a worse shock to him than if he had been used to it. He disliked eating meat for a year after that, although before, he had liked it so much he had been nicknamed '*Bwana Nyama*' ('Sir Meat'), and only recovered his appetite for it when the children had built a full-sized Red Indian 'tepee' on the lawn from blankets and long bamboo poles cut at the river. Indians ate meat, so lumps of cold, roast impala were taken into the tepee and consumed with enthusiasm by the girls. Murray gave in and finding that he enjoyed meat after all, demolished extraordinary quantities of it. He at once felt the benefit.

Guy quite often took the children to the yards when he was working with the cattle, and this encouraged Laria's love of, and interest in, the cattle. He also took them out for rides on the horses, in the bush.

Laria kept snails in a large plastic basin with suitable greenery planted fresh every day, and a net over the top. She observed them and discovered first hand many extraordinary things about them. When she went away for her first term at boarding school, the snails went too. This was no passing interest for she kept snails until she was thirteen, and wrote a beautifully illustrated note-book on their habits. Now in her twenties, she still has a soft spot for snails.

All three children are artistic and from the time they could hold chalk, pencil and brush, spent many happy hours drawing and painting. As there were few shops where toys could be bought and we seldom went to Nairobi, we made nearly all of them ourselves. Before birthdays and Christmas I would make soft-toys: marabou storks and giraffes, pied crows and leopards – even, upon Murray's special request, a vulture. I used scraps left over from dressmaking or chair-cover and curtain making, of which there was a plentiful supply, for I always made everything for the house, and clothes for the children and myself.

Although I have spent much time sewing for the household with a hand-turned machine, I have not often tackled men's tailoring. Not that Guy has ever really minded what he looks like. He has a

Goat being weighed

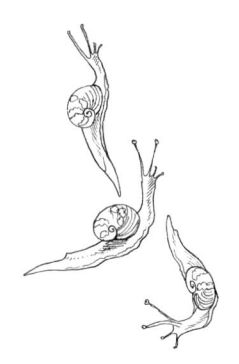

Laria's snails

Indians on a raid

beard because he once calculated that it took him 60 hours out of each year, simply shaving – and now it protects his face from the sun, of which he has had an overdose during his life. He has always worn heavy leather sandals of his own design, which look like footwear found in some archaeological dig. A large-brimmed hat, rather baggy shorts, and, over his shirt, a khaki waist-coat full of strangely shaped buttoned pockets, completes his usual turnout. When it is cold he drapes his head and shoulders with an old kikoi (a traditional striped men's cloth), so that he appears somewhat like an Arab patriarch who has forgotten to don the usual flowing nether garments.

From an early age the children, too, learnt how to make things for themselves. They built doll's houses out of cartons, and all the furniture for them: bookshelves with tiny books of folded paper, framed looking-glasses of silver tinfoil, beds with minute patchwork quilts and rope ladders from windows. But the 'dolls' were toy mice, also made by themselves, which acted out many stories. We made wooden ox-carts pulled by papier mâché oxen which we dried in the oven; and sock-headed hobby-horses. Laria, always particularly interested in the cattle, herded red and white cows she had made from ant-hill clay, upon the lawn, and 'milked' them early every morning. (The 'milk' was water whitened with a little Dettol). Toy-making was a satisfying outlet for creative feelings and we thought that, if ever we fell on hard times, we would have a toy shop in which everything would be made by ourselves.

Laria's clay cows

Almost every day of the year we went out into the bush, first of all pushing the big old-fashioned pram with its fringed canopy before me across country, then, when all the children could walk, unencumbered. Always they saw the wild animals and perhaps they thought the whole world was full of zebras, eland, impala, Grant's gazelles, monkeys, and all the other creatures that we still see every day. In the distance were the Lolldaiga hills, sometimes roller-wing blue, sometimes inky, aquamarine or cobalt. When at last we visited them Murray was disappointed to find that they were coloured just like the rest of the land, and no longer blue.

Sometimes, after a day or two of heavy rain we would set out under the washed, clean sky, each child with a small basket, to find mushrooms. They would run joyfully from one white object to the next and often they were mushrooms, but sometimes only small bones or white flowers. Ahead of them the Crowned plovers, flaunting their black and white-striped wings against the new green grass, steepled into the air with harsh gull-like cries. From a great height came the songs of the Pectoral-patch cisticolas, like the edges of shillings rubbed together, quickening as the little birds in their courtship displays dived breakneck to the ground. Every now and again the children came together to peer into each other's baskets at the mushrooms, the very smallest of which were flushed delicately pink underneath, instead of brown.

When Murray was four he set out one rainy afternoon with a net on a pole to catch a mess of flying termites. He had noticed how much the insects were enjoyed by all the birds and many other creatures. Finding the termites unappetising raw, the children fried a panful. But though delectably crisp, the insects tasted of little more than the butter in which they had been fried.

Occasionally we went to the river to slide down a steep hippo path of black clay, slickened with buckets of water. Laria and Bella would shoot down it like otters and were soon black from head to foot. But Murray kept sticking because he had so little weight, and would become frustrated.

We tried to teach the children not to scamper heedlessly through the bush but to notice everything. One afternoon I nearly trod on a young Black-necked spitting-cobra, four feet long. There was a horrible moment when its head went up so near and I saw from above, the spreading of its hood. I made a huge leap backwards without being aware of doing it. The snake watched us with its head raised, looking like some strange black flower, full of menace. It was a good lesson for the children who had been running about wildly just a little earlier.

When the children were small there was a bad year for rabies, and diseased jackals and Bat-eared foxes appeared in the garden and back yard (and even twice inside the house) with frightening regularity. When we saw one of these animals standing in the mid-day sun with the sinister charisma of the disease upon it, I would hurry the children and dogs inside and shut the doors and windows. We would warn the house staff not to go out. Then Guy would shoot the

Crowned plover

Murray catching termites

THE CHILDREN 57

Rungus

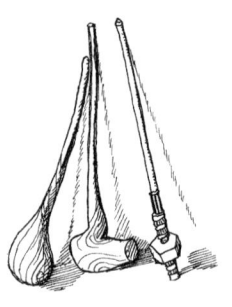

unfortunate animal or, if he was away, one of the men would bravely hit it over the head with his 'rungu' (club). Anxiety communicated itself to the children, and Murray, in particular, used to have nightmares about rabid animals.

Each Christmas we had, as we still have, a 'tree' of dusky leaved kei-apple cut from the hedge and decorated with brightly painted whistling thorn galls, gilded acacia pods and the usual assorted bric a brac collected over many Christmases. It was an exciting occasion, the choosing of a suitable branch and the decorating of it. One year Laria had sprained her ankle but not wishing to miss the choosing, we took her round the hedge in a wheelbarrow. We have a homemade crib with figures of ant-hill clay, some of which were made by the children when they were very young. These Christmas outings of the crib usually end in casualties, but each year new things were made and added so that the crib had its own evolution. And still, when the candles are lit all around, the little figures in the thatched cardboard stable seem to take on a silent, holy magic. The star of Bethlehem and constellations of silver paper, stuck to a deep blue Somali shawl behind, glimmer and twinkle like real stars; and the shepherds and the wise men draw near with reverence.

The Crib

58   ON A KENYA RANCH

SWALLOWS

Swallows swimming gently in rain cleansed air
Are late on their journey North,
And stay to fatten on flying fare.
Have they heard there is snow in Europe
Tardily brushing the landscape, cold?
Here, there are huge white clouds
And the landscape is gold.

Walking in The Bush

Sometimes we are asked if we are afraid to walk alone in the bush, unarmed. We never have been, but wherever possible I avoid places full of thick undergrowth and trees where it is impossible to see ahead. Perhaps that is why I have never felt in danger, apart from an occasional fright. Guy and Murray, who often have to go into areas I avoid, are usually armed, however.

Eland cows

There were two occasions when I got too near to hippopotamuses, which can be very dangerous. The first time I had felt that something was around, and was walking carefully, looking about alertly but not, for some reason, looking ahead. There was a shiny black ant-hill in the path which I did not remember seeing before, so when close to it I looked at it properly. It was a large, wet hippopotamus. I turned and ran back as fast as possible to where Laria had stopped by a tree. 'Quick! Run!' I panted: 'A hippo!'. 'I know' she laughed. The hippo was just where he was before and did not seem interested in chasing us. Laria said I had run just like an ostrich, holding my skirt above my long white legs; and we stood there weak with laughter. On the other occasion I was alone at the river, standing on flat waterside rocks with thick bushes behind, admiring the light and feeling the mysterious and beautiful presence of peace. On moving slowly away up the bank my hat blew off. I stooped with an exclamation to retrieve it. At the sound of my voice a hippo bellowed in the bushes against which I had stood. He must have been watching

A large hippo

with his small piggy eyes, standing stock still himself and feeling, perhaps, that there was no danger in spite of the breeze which blew my scent straight to him – until I gave out a human sound. But by then I was safely up the bank.

Often, it seems that the sound of a voice settles one's identity most clearly in the minds of animals (even in the minds of dogs that know one well), and Murray had a narrow squeak which illustrated this. It was his sixteenth birthday. The family were walking to a part of the river where there is a rock bar which forms a natural weir across it, and I was to drive there later to join them with a picnic. On the way the young became spread out with the dogs divided between them. Murray was with Vortrix, walking quietly along the flank of the second gully, when they heard baboons above them on the ridge. 'Vorty' moved off to investigate and Murray spoke firmly to restrain him. At the sound of his voice a buffalo bull came barging out of a patch of thick croton bush in front of Murray, and stood for a second looking at him. In the same instant Murray swung himself into a tree and the buffalo turned and galloped off down the slope. Murray wondered if the girls would meet the buffalo as he was not sure where they were. By the time I arrived at the river, he was still feeling the effects of the rush of adrenaline that had coursed through him. But it was two years later before I discovered just how close this 'shave' had been. We were walking in the area when Murray said casually: 'This is where I met that buffalo'. I asked him which tree he had climbed, and he indicated a mere sapling. The fork in which he had stood was not three feet from the ground. The wall of croton bushes from which the buffalo had burst forth was so near to the sapling that there was hardly turning room for a buffalo's length. The animal must have realised Murray was not dangerous and, as he had no grudge against mankind, being whole in wind and limb, he went on his way surprised but not angry.

Olive baboon and child

Galloping Buffaloes

Another instance of animals reacting to the human voice was when a friend, setting out on foot to visit us, came upon a herd of elephants, mostly cows and calves, spread over a wide area across his path. It would have increased the length of his journey considerably to detour the herd and as the sun was very hot, he tried shouting instead. The cows and calves moved off but a big bull came straight for him. He had to run for his life, dropping his night-bag as he fled. The elephant paused only to pick this up and fling it to one side. Our friend arrived at the house still shaking, in need of brandy. He told us he had had to run very fast to escape.

The other day, Isabella (now grown up), while passing below the house-dam wall, was knocked down and run over by a family of warthogs which, at the sound of her voice, shot out of a newly dug hole beside her. There was time only for a small shriek from myself before Bella was on her feet again, laughing shakily, and the pigs had disappeared. They made no attempt to bite. Not so long ago a man died from loss of blood after being slashed by a warthog, and one of our employees spent time in hospital after his leg was sliced open by one.

Warthogs

One of the pleasures of walking in the bush of El Karama is the occasional finding of a treasure; perhaps the emerald breast feather of a parrot, long narrow tail plume of a roller, or huge mottled primary of a Kori bustard (said to be the heaviest of all flying birds in the world). Sometimes it might be obsidian flakes worked by pre-historic man, a bright glass bead, porcupine quill, or the curved ivory tusk of a warthog. We have even found two or three 'sucking stones'. These are small stones which have been sucked by pastoralist people to reduce feelings of thirst in dry weather, when water might be limited, or far away. The stones, mostly used by women, are sometimes passed down from mother to daughter for generations, and from much sucking become wonderfully smooth and shiny. They must often be lost or swallowed accidentally however. Occasionally we have found round, faceted quartz balls, whose prehistoric use I do not know. Once they were thought to have been 'bolas' attached to leather thongs for throwing and entangling the legs of animals (as in South America), but that theory has been exploded. Were they simply 'throwing stones' or grinding stones? Or could they have

Kori bustard display

been used in the manufacture of obsidian and bone tools – or for breaking marrow bones? Or perhaps they were simple weapons to be carried. I have felt safer while carrying one.

Another as yet unsolved and, to me, fascinating mystery surrounds a hill-top meadow near our Northern boundary, upon which stands a small, circular, open-topped water tank, its cement weathered to a granular texture by many years of exposure to hot sun and storm. There is no pipe to the tank, as there may once have been from the river, which is over half a mile away down the wooded hillside. From the area surrounding the tank are wonderful views to the East, South and West, although that to the West is less extensive being cut off by the escarpment of Combretum. We watched from the tank once, a young lion on a rock of the escarpment, for an hour before dark, as he lay surveying his hunting grounds. Buffalo often graze on the meadow, and on another smaller one a little farther along the same ridge; they can sometimes be seen in the wooded Chui Luggah below.

Hidden in the grass near the tank are traces of the foundation of a tiny rectangular, round-ended building. Whenever we are there I search for clues to the history of this place; and there are many. Jet-black worked obsidian flakes attest to prehistoric occupation of the site. The hill must always have been a lookout from which wild animals could be observed, and from which the approach of possible enemies could be watched, but above all it must always have been a place of a kind that appeals to man.

Very much more recent than the obsidian flakes on this hilltop are pieces of china – chips of plates banded in yellow, blue or lilac; pieces of saucers, of cups and ornaments decorated with tiny flowers, willow pattern, or lustre – one piece bearing the legend 'made in England'. There are so many fragments, with such a variety of decoration, that it seems someone must have lived there a considerable time to have had so many breakages! A green and a yellow bead, and two small china pans for water colours (with 'Rowney Elementary Colour' stamped on the bottom) were special finds; but green glass from broken wine bottles can be picked up everywhere, and small pieces of flat, thin glass that may have been from window panes. In a gully not far off lie the spoke wheels, bent and rusty, of an old-fashioned car; and a chunk of thick, red glass from a broken tail light. Pieces of cast iron stove top, roof nails and other bits of rusty metal sometimes appear on the bare spaces made by harvester ants, or on the track which leads past the meadow. There seems to be some gentle presence about the hilltop which speaks through each of these small relics. We would like to know more. But although we have asked some of the oldest inhabitants of the district, no-one seems to remember who it was that lived there, in the tiny house (or

Lilac-breasted roller

Ant-hill den

perhaps in tents) – drinking wine with meals, tea from fine china cups, and painting in water-colours. The only person living there now is a White-tailed mongoose, who has his den in the middle of the meadow. And, of course, the birds which nest in the thorn trees nearby; the many insects in the grass.

Whilst walking one afternoon on Combretum, we came out onto the top of a huge rock, and below was the little Suguroi flowing through a grassy glade, shaded by trees. In the grass moved a pack of thin, rough-coated dogs. They slunk off as we and our dogs came down onto the level. A short distance upstream under the bank of an ox-bow, we found two bulging sugar sacks, each filled with chunks of fresh meat. There was a knife still stuck in one of the chunks. Slabs of ribs leant against the bank and some way off lay the head of a waterbuck. We had surprised poachers in the act of cutting up their kill, and we had no doubt they were not far off. A small brown bitch appeared, creeping towards the meat. I threw her a piece which she gobbled gratefully.

Guy had his rifle and decided to lay an ambush. After we others had walked away, talking normally and trying to appear relaxed as if we had noticed nothing, he found himself a hiding place overlooking the ox-bow, backed with rock and brush. Sometime later a single man appeared from upstream and picking up one of the sacks, walked unconcernedly straight towards the ambush. He was momentarily terrified when Guy stood up with the rifle, dropping the sack and putting his hands above his head. He blurted his name and the names of the people he had been with, and Guy wrote them down, but these names later turned out to have been the invention of a quick mind. After he had recovered somewhat, the man claimed the meat had come from a lion's kill, so when Murray and a friend returned an hour later with a vehicle to collect the meat, he was told to show them where this kill had taken place. Leading the way with alacrity he came to a place where a lion had, indeed, recently killed a waterbuck. But lying with the rest of the fresh bones was a waterbuck's head. When he saw how he had confounded himself the poacher availed himself of the opportunity to run off, disappearing instantly among the trees. Even he had not the face to claim this waterbuck had two heads! We discovered later that this man was involved with others in a regular business of poaching and selling meat.

We walk most often in the late afternoon, when the heat is going out of the sun and its rays begin to slant. Then the light is at its most beautiful, sometimes seeming to shine from inside the tawny cloak of the land. When part of the sky is deep plumbeous blue with storm, the grassland is brilliant gold against it. Sometimes an amber light infuses the clouds and makes hazy curtains of rain appear almost brown, and the Red-oat grass is lit in glowing patches. The grass stems shine as they lean and swish in the wind, like a forest of fairy fishing rods. In dry weather, the grey and lichen-rimed trees are fretted with silver outlines against the evening light.

But perhaps even more lovely, though short-lived, is the freshness of the early mornings, when the moon still hangs in the pale sky like a translucent seed husk, and the land is green, and crisped with dew. When the acacias are covered with a creamy froth of blossom the first warmth of the sun fills the cool air with their scent. Or a cold breeze from the south whips the water into your eyes, and the land is so bright and fresh, you feel you could fly.

During the rains we quite often get caught out in storms. There is a sound as of hurrying feet rustling nearer through the bushes, thudding on the bare places, until suddenly rain is falling all around. The heavy drops soak icily through one's shirt, as colour goes out of the landscape to be replaced with grey. The ground turns white with sky-reflecting wetness, and the dogs laugh beside us as we race for the house.

Red oat grass

Impala

WALKING IN THE BUSH **65**

VODKA

Was it meet that you were felled
Untimely, by a leopard's paw,
Before age made you slow?
Dark-eyed spirit, serpent-backed, supple-necked –
You flew, and snatched
Hares from the air as you passed.

How did ordinary dogs convene their genes
To make a Sprite like you?
Now our walks have lost their point –
Hares go unscathed. Surely
There could not be more joy in Heaven,
For dogs, than you felt here?

You pushed Speed to its limit!
Did you fly thus, even to your death?
I pray to the God of fallen sparrows
That you knew little of it,
And ran straight to the plains Beyond:
The joyful Hunting Grounds.

Animal Stories

Dogs

There have been dogs living with us for so long, that sometimes it almost feels that we have become dogs ourselves, and we are certainly members of a pack. Our dogs are also 'people', and they often feature in our dreams, as important-seeming as the human characters therein. There is usually a pack at the house, and there are the other dogs out with the stock, leading useful and hardy lives in

Sambu

the bush. There have been three separate occasions when human lives have been saved by our dogs, once by Naibor and twice by Sambu. All three of these rescues were after attacks by buffaloes.

Naibor's rescue has already been described in 'A Small Piece of Africa'. Sambu, a Staffordshire bull terrier-cross, saved the life of a friend of Murray's from South Africa, David, who was attacked by a buffalo bull on another ranch after he had run past a thicket in which three bull buffaloes were dozing. Sambu had been persuaded to accompany this cross-country run. When David, a pentathlete who had competed internationally, realised the buffalo was coming for him, he ran for a tree, but before he could reach it he fell. The buffalo galloped over him, stepping on his inner thigh, cleaving muscle from bone and exposing the femoral artery. The buffalo then turned and hooking him on one horn by the buttock, spun him round and round 'like a rag doll', threw him into the air over its shoulder, and charged him again. This time it hit a rock beside which David had landed, enabling him to use his feet to push off

The buffalo was coming for him!

from the buffalo's boss each time it tried to gore him. But he felt himself losing consciousness, and the buffalo would almost certainly have killed him if Sambu had not attracted its attention to himself by biting and barking, and lured it off into the bush. Murray, in running to the place where he had heard David scream, met another bull and had to dive into a thicket of thorns. He then bandaged David's frightful wounds as well as he could with his shirt, while someone else brought a vehicle to the spot. This took a while as the accident occurred in an isolated and hilly area with no track. Later, Sambu caught up with the vehicle as it was speeding to the airstrip, and taking a flying leap into the back of it he inspected David's leg, licked his face, and finding him still alive and able to speak, sat down companionably on his head. David was flown in the dark, then driven, to Nanyuki, where he received a hundred and fifty stitches after an hour and a half of cleaning, all without anaesthetic. Being very fit, it did not take him long to recover completely, except for a very slight limp.

Sambu may also have saved Murray's life, from a buffalo cow. Murray and a friend were walking in the Carisia Hills, which can be seen on a clear day from El Karama. The cow charged out of a thicket at point blank range. Brushing past Elliot, who instinctively turned towards a tree trunk, she swept Murray up on one horn, the tip of which was lodged under his ribs. He had time to think as he was carried along, 'This horn is in a very dangerous place', when providentially he was brushed off by branches, and fell to the ground. Sambu made sure the cow did not return, and Murray suffered nothing more than a badly sprained knee, a bruise under his ribs and a tear in his shirt. Elliot said the buffalo looked like a gigantic grey pig as it shot past him. For a few seconds he and the Samburu man they were with did not realise why Murray had disappeared. They found him lying, temporarily shocked, about twenty yards away in the thick forest. Murray recalled afterwards that it had been like being hit by a speeding Landcruiser.

It was not very long after this incident that, tragically, Sambu disappeared without trace one night, presumably killed and carried off by a leopard, on another ranch where Murray was working at the time.

※

Jimmy Asali, a sandy mongrel, was probably a honey-hunter's dog. He was found wandering alone on El Karama with a wire round his neck, many years ago now; thin, unkempt, and covered with ticks and fleas. We were struck by his personality, and, after he had been cleaned and well fed, he became a boma dog with one of the herds. He gave years of loyal service, carrying himself always with dignity, humour and self-possession. Though rather small he was game for a

Each kennel also has a walled run at back

fight and once took on six dogs, all twice his size, at one time. Some of Asali's grandchildren still guard the herds and flocks of El Karama, and his great grandchildren are growing up now. Years later this line was joined by that of another dog out of the bush. Mwitu (from '*mbwa mwitu*' – African Hunting Dog in Swahili) was a poacher's dog who arrived at the house of his own volition. He was obviously part Alsatian, tall and dark, but terribly thin and weak. As soon as we saw each other we felt a bond of sympathy, and Mwitu became my shadow. On walks he would return ridiculously often to make sure I was all right; and he responded to good food and a healthy life, soon becoming a fine dog. But the trauma of early neglect had damaged his liver, and by the end of his second year with us he began to lose his appetite. Eventually he became so weak he had to be put down. But he left his mate, Worra, with a litter of fine puppies. His son 'Vorty' (Vortrix) became my special dog. Worra, and their daughter Tinka, with admixtures of Staffordshire bull terrier, Blue heeler and pointer, have gone on to produce our present pack.

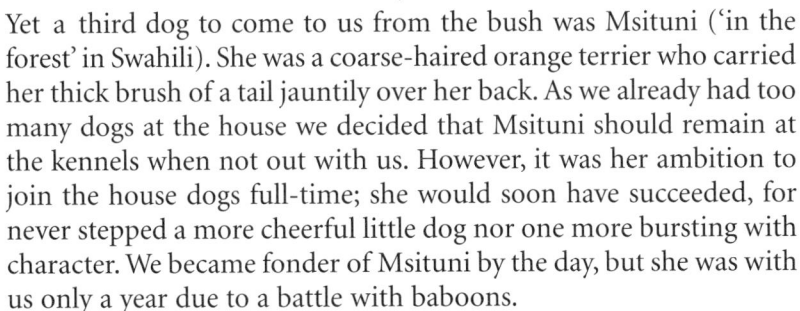

Jimmy Asali

❋

Yet a third dog to come to us from the bush was Msituni ('in the forest' in Swahili). She was a coarse-haired orange terrier who carried her thick brush of a tail jauntily over her back. As we already had too many dogs at the house we decided that Msituni should remain at the kennels when not out with us. However, it was her ambition to join the house dogs full-time; she would soon have succeeded, for never stepped a more cheerful little dog nor one more bursting with character. We became fonder of Msituni by the day, but she was with us only a year due to a battle with baboons.

The dogs had hurried ahead as we set out for an afternoon walk, and hearing baboons in the first gully below the house, we stopped to call them back. Suddenly we heard the unmistakable sounds of battle. Running as fast as we could, we rounded some bushes to see Msituni sitting groggily in the grass, red with blood. Baboons were running off, followed by the other dogs. As we bent over her, a terrible howl rose above the general babel of barking dogs and baboons. It

Msituni

was the voice of Towseler. We ran on, leaving Msituni. We passed a huge male baboon lying dead in the gully. I thought Towseler would be dead, too. Eventually we found him on his side in a patch of scrub, gashed and shocked. The baboons had withdrawn, but in case they came back one of the children stayed with Towseler, while another ran to call for a vehicle, and I returned to Msituni, who was

Olive Baboons

by then weak from loss of blood. I tried to hold the worst wound together to stop the bleeding, but by the time we had got her into the car and back to the verandah, and MtuAburuki had sewn up her wounds she was too weak to move – though she made a feeble but obvious effort to get inside the house. I ignored this because we had to go back to the gully with hurricane lamps (for by now it was dark) to stitch Towseler's wounds. When we returned, exhausted, with Towseler on an improvised stretcher, Bella warned me that Msituni was 'not all right'. She had died there on the back verandah for lack of proper veterinary treatment, within reach of her goal; and I will always regret not honouring her wish to die inside the house. Msituni was buried in the garden. We wanted to give the baboon, who had died defending his troop, honourable burial too; but in the morning the body had disappeared; presumably carried off by a leopard. Although we had not seen what had happened, it is almost certain that the dogs had started this fight by attacking the baboons.

But normally El Karama is perhaps as near to Paradise for dogs as anywhere could be. There are always astute hares to be chased over the wide, free land, and nearly caught but not quite – so that usually they live to be chased again. The dogs seem unaware of dangers so that their lives are unclouded by anxiety. The other day they streamed past a huge puff-adder which was lying like a log on a patch of bare ground. Its head and neck were doubled back along its body, ready to strike. Wasp, Sambu's daughter, passed within two feet of it. I called her away but, sensing from my voice that I had seen something exciting and dangerous, Wasp turned back to investigate. To my horror she passed within striking distance of the snake again without seeing it. It never moved!

Sometimes the dogs get too close to warthogs, meeting a group of them, perhaps, under a shady wait-a-bit bush specially hollowed out inside by the pigs as a cool retreat. Then the dogs risk being

Boma dog in 44-gallon-drum kennel

gashed by slashing lower tushes. We train them to leave warthogs and the equally dangerous baboons alone, but occasionally they succumb to temptation. Vodka, who had gone out hunting with other dogs on their own (a thing they do not normally do), was killed and eaten by a leopard – only her white tail, a few fragments of bone, and tracks left to tell us what had happened.

Because it is so sad to lose them, there are times when I wish we had no dogs. It is also difficult for me to control properly more than two dogs at a time, but as it is often necessary to take at least five out together, our walks sometimes turn into hunts during which it is impossible to prevent an occasional tragedy when other animals are killed.

Potential disasters do not always happen, however, as we are often able to prevent them. The dogs saw a very small waterbuck calf in the long grass to one side of the airstrip, and galloped towards it. Luckily I was not far away, and managed to arrive at nearly the same moment. Because I was there, with my arms round the calf (which did not try to run away) the dogs listened to my commands of 'No', and 'Go home!' I stayed with the calf until the dogs were half way along the strip on their way home, then left it unhurt to be collected later by its mother, who had obviously concealed it in the long grass between suckling visits, as it was still very young.

There is the risk of tick-borne diseases for the dogs, and they must be washed every week with pyrethrum insecticidal shampoo to keep ticks away. Even so, and in spite of treatment, we have lost one or two dogs to Rickettsia. If the illness is noticed early and treated at once, they usually recover however.

❉

His mother was half Border collie, half Australian Blue heeler. His father was a big brown mongrel. But Jake followed the Blue heeler branch of his family, having a stout black and white body and a wide head set off by pricked ears. He was born with his tail bent downwards and as this gave him problems, it was later docked by a vet. This short tail gave him a spurious air of being some special breed, and people often asked admiringly what he was. He was a rascal. He knew he was not supposed to get on beds, but he also knew that I was weak about this. He would climb up and settle down comfortably – but if he heard Guy approach, he would get off immediately and be doing something quite different by the time he arrived. I wish our present dogs were as tactful!

Though he was a very small puppy when we first saw him, four-square and solemn, with the hair of his back standing up woolly and rough, he was full of friendly confidence and would swagger up to towering strangers to give a friendly caper or two. Once, when greeting a visitor enthusiastically, he fell on his back into a narrow

Warthog's daytime retreat

Waterbuck calf

Jake

concrete drain in which his small, fat body fitted exactly, and had to be rescued while we tried not to laugh.

When Jake grew up he understood I was interested in birds, and whenever I stopped to focus binoculars he would wait beside me until I lowered them, then trot forward to flush the bird and sniff where it had been. Sometimes he would watch birds with interest himself, following their progress through branches with sparkling eyes. Once, hearing him barking excitedly, I found him staring at a pair of Pied crows in the top of a tree: 'towny' birds which neither of us had seen on El Karama before. They were some distance away, but Jake had apparently recognised them at once as something new.

Towny birds (Pied crows)

Jake always entered eagerly into the spirit of whatever was going on. When the children were practising gymnastics one afternoon, running and turning somersaults onto a mattress on the lawn, Jake, who had been watching, also ran at the mattress and taking the edge of it in his teeth, flung his body over in a somersault. It was not, perhaps, in the best style, but we were astonished. Later, the children held the mattress above his head and he was jumping under it, trying to bite it. Higher and higher they lifted the mattress, higher and higher jumped Jake, twisting in the air in his efforts to tear it. Guy, disturbed by the laughter and barking, opened his office window and called – 'His manners are bad enough without you making them worse!'. Jake stopped jumping instantly and slunk, shamefaced and silent with the children, into the house. It was comical to see such similar expressions of embarrassment in the attitudes of children and dog.

Jake loved football and joined in our family games with enthusiasm, dribbling the ball expertly in front of him, though uncertain which side he was playing for; and tearing up and down stopping balls with a thump, against his wide chest. Sometimes he bit the ball and had to be banished to the verandah from where he would watch with vicarious eagerness until he could bear it no longer, and rushed out again to join in.

Jake would lead me, my skirt held in his teeth; and when preparing to set out on a walk he often bashed my shins with the boot he would be excitedly shaking. He resented other dogs being in front of him on walks but, as most of them had longer legs than he did, it was hard to keep them behind. His black and white body hurtling along, he would growl and bite if they tried to pass him; but usually they succeeded anyway. If, while on a walk, you sat down, perhaps to sketch or watch animals, Jake would sit with his back pressed against yours facing in the opposite direction. From this position he would warn you if anything came near. But sometimes he would get tired of waiting and take himself home.

We had a big, good natured pointer called Sprottles, whom Jake

Worra   Pirate
Jake's puppies

The River Uasso Nyiro

Sept '95.

Feb '93.

In dung.

Sept '95.

Watercolour paint made from spores of tent-peg fungus + thin glue & water.
Raw umber.

Hard, woody stipe, like tent-peg. Cap covered with saffron-brown "powder" (spores on outside). Made considerable upheaval of hard earth at plantation.

Some fungi

Muscovy duck with ducklings

1978 Laria, Bella, Murray and Esther with kids

Bush fire as seen from El Karama

Dry weather fires beyond the Three Hills

Our old tractor

View in Nanyuki 1976

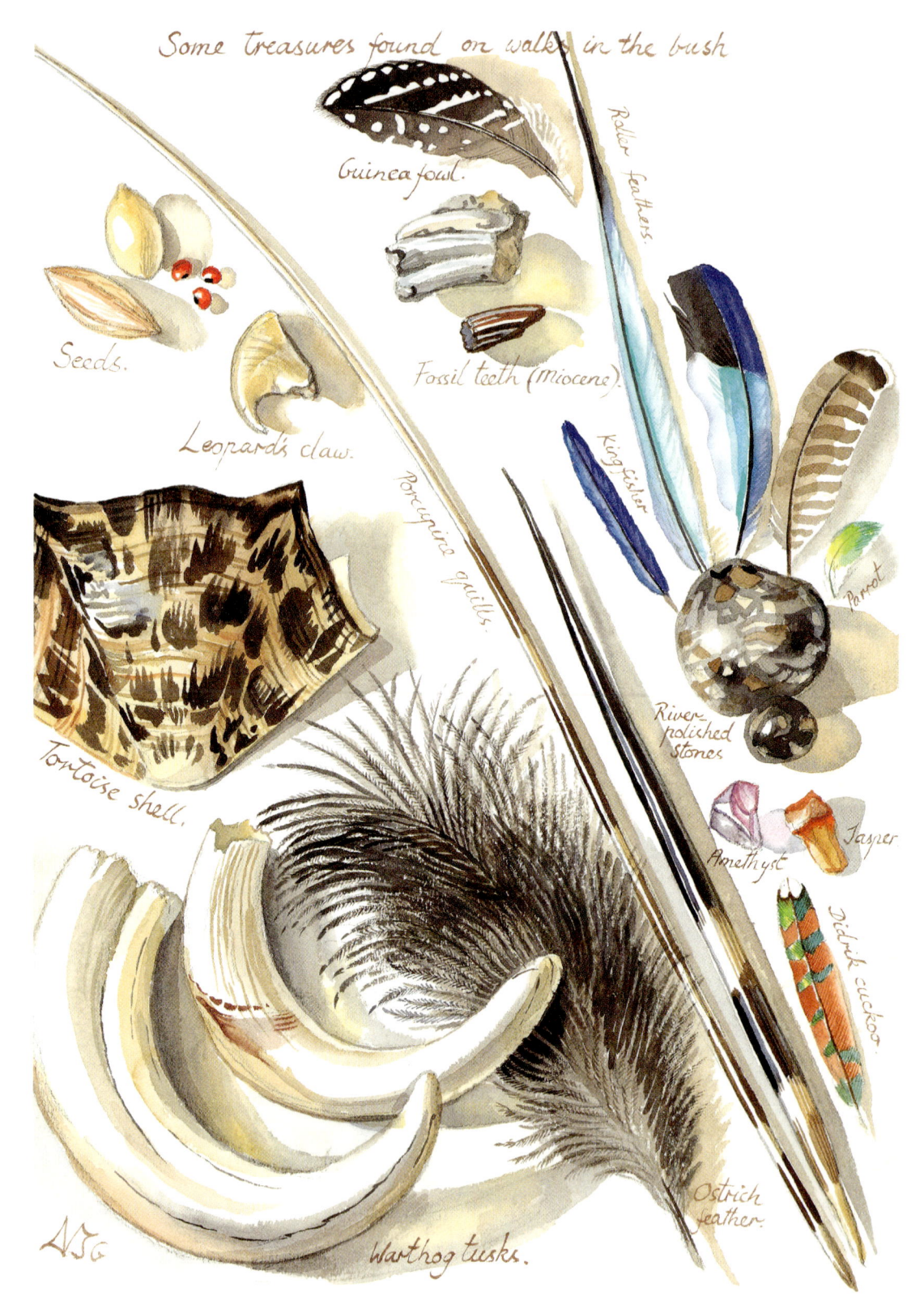

Some treasures found on walks in the bush

More treasures found in the bush

Verandah bedroom with Bhageera on bed

The Orchard, looking over Lucerne and wired-in garden to mare's stable. Bonar grass to right, Sept. 2000

imagined to be an arch rival. Every three months or so Jake would attack 'Sprot' and there would be a brief and bloody fight. But, 'Sprot' being much the bigger dog, the fights always ended by his immobilising Jake; either held by the throat, or, which was even more ignominious, by the scruff. 'Sprot' was not vindictive. There would be peace for a few months while Jake's wounds healed, until he once again forgot that it was impossible to beat 'Sprot'.

Jake held the position of court jester in our family, as he so often made us laugh. One day he rolled accidentally down the steep river bank, his bolster-shaped body speeding his descent to a terrific splash. He did not really like water, avoided swimming and hated his weekly bath – so this sudden ducking disorientated him and he came out on the wrong bank. But how odd he looked! Water had got into one of his ears and his head was so far on one side as to be almost upside-down, as he staggered this way and that like a drunken bee. It took us a long time to persuade him to re-enter the water and swim back, and meanwhile he stared at us gloomily. He was very pleased when he finally managed to rejoin us, and at once found the stickiest patch of mud and rolled in it joyfully until he was brown all over, his fur congealed into prickly-looking spikes. Then he found a rotting carcase, rolled in that, and carried a bone jauntily for the rest of the walk. That is what he thought of swimming, and of cleanliness in general.

It is often inconvenient to take dogs in the car, but Jake loved car rides and was always depressed when left behind. On an occasion when we had to make a call from the nearest telephone – miles away – we left Jake behind, as we thought, with a firm command for the dogs to 'stay'. When we were six miles from the house there was a scuffle behind the front seats and Jake clambered onto the back seat, looking pleased with himself. He knew we were now too far from the house to return him, as we had on previous occasions of his stowing away when he had been discovered earlier.

For recreation Jake enjoyed being with me and the children; but his real work was ranching. He had a natural instinct for herding and loved helping with the sheep and goats, and nipping the heels of cattle at suitable moments. He would follow Guy to the office, the yards, the stables and the paddocks, and his conspicuous black and white form was a reliable pointer to Guy's whereabouts. If Guy accidentally gave him the slip, Jake would 'hoover' fast about the garden, his nose glued to the ground and emitting loud snorts, until he found the scent trail and invariably discovered where Guy was.

Jake died of Rickettsia when he was five, and though we missed him with painful intensity for a long time, we remember him now with happiness for the fun he gave us.

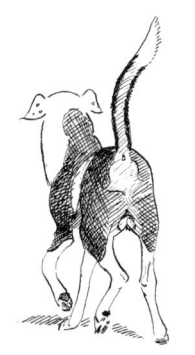

Toru, Son of Jake

Striped ground-squirrel

ANIMAL STORIES

THE GRÉVY'S ZEBRA STALLION

In the middle of the night a
Grévy's zebra brayed.
He was on the green outside
The ruined house.
His voice took possession of the
World, the damp air;
So loud and deep, magnificent,
That Hengist the Jackass
Stood silent in his stall –
Mighty was the sound!
It was as a bass trumpet
Wynded there;
And between the trembling blasts
The indrawn breath
Made funny little squeaks.

Horses

As a child I put pocket money into a Post Office savings account in order to buy a pony. I drew a picture of a pony divided into small squares which represented pound notes, and half squares for the ten shilling notes. These were coloured in over a number of years, until one day the whole animal was resplendent in red, orange, blue, green, pink and yellow. (Of the greater costs of stabling and feeding I was happily unaware). But at the very time when 'my' pony seemed at last about to materialise, we moved to London. That was the end of ponies for me until El Karama. Then there was all, and more than I could ask for, of horses – even Arab stallions, which had been the fabulous lodestone of childhood day-dreams.

❈

The El Karama bloodline started with Guy's first stallion Tallal Shagyar, a grey Arab-Lipizzaner, and Kisima, a bright bay half Somali mare whom he brought with him when he first came here. Kisima, sired by the Powys's Arab, Prodigal, was descended on her dam's side from Somali ponies brought down in 1945 by Guy's father from Mega in southern Ethiopia, when he had been British Consul there. A significant contribution to the bloodline was also made by a small dun mare, Shirley, who had been caught as a wild pony on the Rumuruti plains, not far from El Karama. Although not much to look at herself, her descendants are among our largest and most beautiful horses (many of them golden buckskin), all with strong constitutions ideally suited to tough conditions. Shirley walked faster than any of the other horses and her descendants have inherited this action.

Tallal Shagyar (with Kiugu)

❈

After Tallal, Guy was given the pure bred Arab stallion, Xenophon, gentle of character, who had previously slipped a stifle joint in an accident, so was permanently lame. Like Prodigal and Tallal he had been bred by F. O. B. Wilson at Kilima Kiu, south of Nairobi. Xenophon was already quite old when I came to El Karama. I used sometimes to put carrots in his feed, which he loved, and go into his loose-box to groom him and massage his lame hip which had stiffened with age. Murray, when only two or three years old, would sometimes sit on his back. Xenophon could open any door including that of his own stable which was fastened with a bolt, so that it had to be secured also with a nut. He would lift the wire loop on the garden gate and enter from his paddock to prance about the lawn and shout his high, brassy neigh to horses by the back yard gate. We then tied the loop down with knotted string, for he could undo bows. He even learnt to slide open the poles of his paddock fence.

Xenophon in garden

Soon after we were married Guy had built me a painting house

The painting house

Maize-crib skin store (with Karama)

Xarifah

of wattle and daub in the stallion's paddock. The wattle is 'mukinyea' poles cut from the bush, the daub is cow dung mixed with clay, thickly applied, finally smoothed with dung and ash, and whitewashed inside and out. The floor was earthen, but grit used to stick to my oil paintings and if one fell face down, a not uncommon occurrence, it was a minor disaster; so the floor was later paved with flat stones from a nearby gully. Sometimes, when I was in my painting house, 'Xen' would come in unexpectedly. The house is too small for a horse to turn round in easily and I was always nervous lest he get a fright and fall, or knock his head on the door frame when going out. Once inside he inspected everything with intelligent interest. He would wiffle his upper lip in the paint on the palette, then smear it clean on the wall. He sniffed the bottles of linseed and turpentine, which I had to pick up off the floor as quickly as possible. Then he would move to the far end of the hut to look at the many things on the shelf there. After this thorough inspection of my strange stable, he would back out slowly and carefully.

Xenophon sired our two present stallions, Karama and Xarifah. Karama is a powerful Anglo-Arab with a red-bay satin coat lit with inner gleams of copper, and a long, black mane and tail. He, too, comes into the painting house if I forget to shut the door, but he is rougher than Xenophon was. He whisks the cushion off the chair and tries to knock the chair itself over; tastes my straw hat, stands on paint tubes, picks up the sheepskin on which I like to sit, and turns impatiently to go out. He leaves at a plunging canter, seeming to strike sparks from the stone floor as he goes. Once he frightened me by coming in when I was painting a still life of glass bottles, arranged on a makeshift shelf in the middle of the hut.

Xarifah, an Arab, is smaller; a flea-bitten grey of grace and lightness of movement. One day an apprentice horseman was leading Xarifah through Karama's paddock to the stables. As usual, Karama had been put away first, but on this occasion his stable door had not been properly shut and he came bounding out. Xarifah fled back to his paddock through the open gates, followed closely by Karama who chased him round and round, blasting trumpet-calls of rage. I thought that if Xarifah stopped he would be killed. Every time they came thundering towards the garden end of the paddock I opened the gate, hoping he would come through and I could then slam it shut on Karama. But Xarifah, half-crazed with fear, had somehow got his head-collar on upside-down so that it partly covered his eyes and he could not see properly. He tried desperately to climb through the garden hedge, full of wicked thorns, while Karama piled up against him, biting savagely. My mouth had gone completely dry with fear: the first time I had known what that means. When Xarifah was slate-coloured with sweat I knew they could not gallop much

Mare's stable

longer. Finally he was cornered at the bottom of the paddock against a pole fence, and from the roars and screams I thought he was being killed. But the horses were too exhausted to fight! The horsemen managed, by opening the bottom poles, to let the little grey through whilst preventing Karama from following.

Xarifah quivered and puffed for an hour while I washed and dressed his wounds. But next day Karama was the stiffer of the two. Being larger, he had found it more difficult to dodge round the trees in the paddock at a gallop.

※

A man on horseback goes out nearly every afternoon of the year visiting each flock and herd of the ranch. He carries instructions to the herdsmen, treats simple sicknesses in the small stock, and brings back reports. His presence acts as a deterrent to stock thieves: they cannot tell where he will turn up, and he can canter home with the alarm if necessary. The horse he rides is one of the twenty-odd, most of whom have been bred, born, brought up and trained on the ranch; and which will grow old and eventually die here. Horses are not sold for they are part of the ranch family.

Horses that are not to be ridden on a particular day are free in the bush and can wander as far as they like. In the evening they usually come home of their own accord and wait at the gate to be let in – but if Kanga, a mule, is with them, she opens the gate herself. Sometimes, when green grass has newly appeared after rain, the horses stay out and have to be searched for. They may be miles away. Then, too, when the earth is softened, they delight in galloping. We hear the rolling thunder of their hooves approaching from far off, louder and louder: then suddenly they appear. With tails flying high and piston legs flickering beneath them, they come up the slope from the First Gully, flat out. Before the gate they mill with tossing heads, snorting from flared nostrils and springing with long strides as they decelerate.

On patrol with Imani

ANIMAL STORIES 77

Patrol. Aburuki on Sirocco

It is noticeable to us that horses, living free, with an extended and almost natural social system of their own, who have never been roughly treated or kept stabled for any length of time, are friendly and entirely without vices towards humans, although they have developed their own 'pecking orders' and friendships amongst themselves which they defend with tooth and hoof. And living a free life in the bush teaches horses to think for themselves, and their intelligence and powers of observation are developed as a result. Seiya, a bay gelding, was once caught by all four feet in a wire fence. Instead of struggling and cutting himself terribly, or desperately banging his head on the ground as most other horses would have done, he lay there quietly until found by someone who, luckily, went

Galloping home

out that way. When freed he had only a few scratches to show for his ordeal. One striking example of observation, was when Muscat, a young chestnut gelding, walked over to me from the far side of the stable boma, between a number of other horses, to look at a narrow woven bracelet I was wearing for the first time. He had noticed it at once, and lowered his head to pull an end of it tentatively. He also enjoys removing Laria's hairband which he does gently, without pulling her hair.

The horses have always been fascinated by camels, and the first time they saw these (on the morning after the family returned from a camel safari in the North) they were wild with excitement. That evening they came in from the bush early, craning over the gate to see the camels again (which had since left). Once the gate was opened they cantered all over the back yard with their heads up, hoping to find them, and were clearly disappointed when they failed to do so. They were also astonished by a small group of pied cattle with long horns, which had been recovered from stock thieves on the ranch, and had been brought in to the yards. It was obvious from their excitement and suspicion, that they did not recognise them as cattle. To them cattle were uniformly coloured creatures without horns – for they had known no others.

Strange cattle

Because of the danger of lions, the horses that are not stabled spend the night in an enclosure behind the house, surrounded by a Kei-apple hedge on two sides and a pole fence on the other. More than once the night-watchman has found an elephant in the enclosure with the horses, which had stepped over the gate in order to enjoy eating a Pepper tree which grows inside. The horses were huddled silently as far away from their tremendous visitor as they could get.

※

It was after a heavy shower of afternoon rain that a strange 'mare' and foal were seen waiting anxiously at the farmyard gate. The foal was a mule, with very long ears and unusual stripey legs: but we found, to our astonishment, that the 'mother' of the foal was a gelding. Furthermore, this gelding was very protective towards the little mule which was far too young to have been weaned. When we tried to catch the foal in order to feed it from a bottle, the gelding thrust himself between us and it. Finally, while we fed it, he pushed up close to make sure no harm came to his charge. So we kept the two together until the gelding, realising that 'his' foal was being looked after, lost interest and went to live with the other horses. Meanwhile, for the next six months, the little mule was given her bottle every two hours or so to begin with, later every four hours, and finally three times a day. Very soon she became attached to Bobby, an old skewbald Shetland pony who shared the paddock. There was no problem while Kanga (short for *Kangani* – Grévy's zebra in Swahili) was still small, for she accompanied us when the children rode on Bobby. But as she grew older she became wilder, barging against Bobby and kicking and biting playfully. So we would leave her in the paddock for the duration of the rides and she would gallop up and down the fence with her floating stride, emitting extraordinary wails. When only half grown she leapt the six-barred paddock gate with astonishing ease. Put in a stable, she immediately jumped out over the half door. Rails were then fitted across the top section of the stable door and, confident that we had solved our problem, Kanga was shut inside. I was in the next-door stable when hearing a noise and looking

The children with Bobby and Kanga

ANIMAL STORIES 79

out, I beheld Kanga slithering through the two-foot gap between the top rail and the roof and, like an eel coming down a waterfall, stretching vertically to the ground. After this we gave up trying to confine her and she accompanied rides led by her own attendant. This arrangement lasted until she was old enough to go out with the main horse herd into the bush during the day, when her attachment to Bobby gradually weakened.

For months after her arrival we tried to discover where Kanga and her protector had come from, so that we might return them to their owner. Eventually we heard that they belonged to Jack Fairhall, a great character who lived some way to the North. He told us that Kanga was the daughter of his mare and a wild Grévy's zebra stallion, which would explain her extraordinary voice and striped legs. Be that as it may, on the morning that they appeared at our gate a lion had killed Kanga's mother and the gelding had run off with the foal and disappeared. Jack said that as we had successfully raised Kanga, we should keep her; and we could buy the horse (whom we named Jet after one of Jack's sons).

We wonder if Jet knew that Kanga's survival depended on his getting her to humans as quickly as possible, or if their arrival at our gate was providential.

After Kanga had gone to live with the horses, Bobby the Shetland acquired a new friend; a black pony called Nangi. No-one knew how old Nangi was, but he had been around as long as anyone in the neighbourhood could remember, being handed on from family to family as children grew out of him.

Nangi and Bobby would sometimes share food from a single bucket. Bobby would snatch a large mouthful, then, jerking his head out of the bucket, would invariably upset it. Nangi, expertly twitching the bucket upright, would take two or three mouthfuls and withdraw his head; when Bobby would take his next mouthful, upsetting the bucket again. This sequence was repeated with the regularity of a pendulum until the food was finished. Then Bobby would open the corral gate by ramming it with his backside, and hurry out looking smug and recalcitrant. But Nangi always managed an expression of detached innocence, although he was extremely sagacious.

Cats

Perhaps partly because we are, in some ways, an isolated community, with none of the city dweller's amusements and distractions and fast pace of social life, which we do not envy, animals as daily companions and friends have come to mean very much to us, for our lives are inextricably intermingled with theirs, and they have enriched ours almost more than anything. So, if to some readers it may seem puzzling why I have written so much about animals, the above must be the explanation of why that is so.

In the house at Combretum lived a small black cat, left behind by the Turkana people, we thought. She must have been there all her life for she was hardly more than a kitten when we took over the place. She was full of poise and quiet self-confidence, always coming to greet us and watching us out of sight when we left – a small inky figure, her eyes like chips of yellow glass, sitting alone outside the back door. Murray called her Ndimu ('lemon' in Swahili) for the colour of her eyes.

At each of our visits Ndimu seemed to be fatter, and one day she did not appear as usual. I called. Although she then came at once, she looked bedraggled, wet and stiff. For a second I thought she was hurt, before realising she had been having kittens. On the back verandah was a yellow plastic container that had once held a gallon of cooking oil, and which had had its top cut off. Inside this small shelter we found three stripey kittens, still wet and unlicked – for Ndimu had answered my call the moment she had finished giving birth. The father of the kittens was an African wild cat, and while still blind they were very fierce, spitting explosively if a hand came near them. Eventually, to our regret, these beautiful kittens went off to live wild in the bush. But by then Ndimu was expecting another family.

Ndimu on Combretum verandah

The three new wild-cat kittens were brought over to El Karama with their mother. We had not tried to bring her previously for fear our many dogs would frighten her away – but at once it was obvious that no dog could frighten Ndimu. It was quite the other way round! She chased them in turn, yelping in terror across the garden and through the house. If any dog so much as looked at one of her kittens, or if a kitten spat, growled or yowled for help, Ndimu came running unhesitatingly to do battle on its behalf.

Once, when bitches were in season and supposed to be shut away, they appeared unexpectedly in the garden closely followed by Sambu. Whilst we tried to keep Sambu away from one bitch and called for someone to remove the other, Ndimu streaked to our rescue and plastered herself by all prickles to Sambu's white front, quenching his ardour instantly. The bitches were hurried away unscathed. Another time Ndimu attacked young Sambu's rear end when he had threatened to chase a foal, and she has broken up many dog fights. Indeed, whenever she hears voices raised in an effort to control dogs, she comes hurrying to see if her help is needed. Sometimes the dogs try to get their own back on Ndimu. Once I saw them advance on her in a line and suddenly, as if at a signal, charge together. But Ndimu stood her ground and they came to a halt in front of

Ndimu about to break up a dog fight

ANIMAL STORIES **81**

her, nonplussed. As they hesitated she charged them, causing an ignominious rout.

Although she knows we go too fast for her, Ndimu sometimes comes for walks, hurrying with the dogs or trailing behind imploring us to go slower. If anyone goes out at night to check, perhaps, a foaling mare, Ndimu goes too, and waits outside the stable at the edge of the lamplight, sitting with the dogs. If Guy does a round with the night watchman Ndimu accompanies him, a shadow blacker than the night, very easy to trip over.

Perhaps Ndimu does not realise how small she is and therefore, how vulnerable. One morning she could not be found, nor for three days afterwards. Then she turned up with a hernia; most of her intestines, it seemed, bulging into the skin of her belly. Strangely, our daughter, Laria, had been diagnosed as having a hernia a few days previously, so she and Ndimu were taken to Nairobi together for their operations. The vet said that Ndimu's hernia had been caused by a dog bite, but the little cat still shows no fear of any of our dogs.

Years before Ndimu, there was Bhageera. He was a big black cat with a tiny white spot on his throat, just like Rudyard Kipling's black panther, Bhageera. For two years we saw his lithe form only fleetingly in the undergrowth. He seemed completely wild and self sufficient, showing little interest in humans except to avoid them. But one evening, there he was on a window ledge, staring in with eyes of peeled-grape green – eyes that seemed wells of utter loneliness and ferocity of a kind for which there could surely be no remedy. Yet from that moment he became, by his own choice, a House Cat. He entered the room, drank a saucer of milk, grappled the ankle of a visitor who tried to touch him, and left. Next afternoon Bhageera came back and this time he stayed for good. Never again did he scratch or bite anyone, except gently in play; though sometimes he would put on savage shows of catching his own tail, to indicate he was hungry. He did not torment other animals and birds: anything he caught was killed instantly and eaten. But once he grabbed a pink balloon which the children had been trying to keep off the floor by batting it around a room. There was a gasp of horrified amusement followed by a pregnant silence as Bhageera clasped the balloon to his chest in his thick black arms, his spread claws dimpling its surface, ears back, hind legs drawn up for a 'disemboweling' kick. We waited for the explosion which would terrify him out of his wits, but it never came. Bhageera, after his pretence at savaging the balloon, gently let it go. He knew about balloons.

Bhageera was a strong cat. We saw him muscling past the sitting-room window from the direction of the kitchen, with a leg of impala swinging from his jaws. His neck was craned back and the shoulders of his braced legs swung in counterpoint to the swing of the meat. It

Tiger and Suguroi (Half-wildcat kittens)

Bella with Bhageera

must have weighed at least as much as he did – perhaps more. It was, I felt, a feat as great in proportion as that of Corbett's tiger which carried a whole ox, in one bound, up a ten foot bank.

It was Bhageera who tackled a rabid Bat-eared fox that entered that part of the verandah where I used to give the children their lessons, and whirled with it, avoiding being bitten, onto the grass outside where he left it to continue its mad pilgrimage round the house.

He resented disturbances in his territory that he had not made himself. One day a serious dog fight of ripping, tearing intensity had erupted under Guy's office window. As I ran out the fight broke off mysteriously in sudden silence. Only the black cat was there, looking smug and perhaps a little surprised. Guy explained that he had galloped across thirty yards of grass and without hesitation leapt on top of the whirling protagonists. They, instantly forgetting their fight, had shot off round the corner of the house.

A mate for Bhageera appeared out of the bush, as he himself had come to us. She was a small, unkempt tabby with sand-coloured, black-edged gecko eyes, whom Laria named Cowrie. We never discovered where either of them came from, but perhaps they had been born in the wild of feral parents. They may even have been descended from Guy's first cat, Cheeky, a Siamese tom whom he had been constrained to give away across the river eighteen years previously. For the families of Cowrie and Bhageera contained beautiful cats of Siamese colouring, and another more like a snow leopard, with brilliant sapphire eyes – the bluest eyes I have seen anywhere. People found it hard to believe they were the offspring of black Bhageera and his little, ordinary-looking mate, Cowrie.

As he grew older Bhageera became more and more my familiar, spending much time on my bed like a pool of Indian ink; or on my knee. Often he stood upright beside me at meals with his claws on the edge of the table, like some benevolent demon. The marks of his claws are still there.

When finally he became ill, he camped out in a flower bed and refused to come in. We built a shelter of mackintoshes over him to keep off rain and wind. He could not eat and became steadily weaker. When I brought him re-hydration drink he sat up and made an attempt to lap, but I felt he was doing it only to please me. Lying down again he appeared very frail, as he slowly rested his head on the soft ground. Later, Guy came to me to say he thought it would be kinder to shoot Bhagie. I agreed. He did it while I waited by the gate to my painting house. It was peaceful there, with snails moving gracefully over the trellis, and a Morning warbler sang a few crystal clear phrases from the hedge nearby. Its song seemed to express utter truth, as if nothing more ever needed to be said.

Cowrie

Black-bellied bustard in flight

ANIMAL STORIES **83**

DRAGONFLIES

Many dragonflies, dull brown,
Are passing; flittering busy things;
Pausing here, diving down,
Rising, whirring on hovering wings.
They are hunting like aerial sharks.
But between the sun and me
These dragonflies are not the same!
Each as it passes turns to fire;
It's flexy body, pencilled in flame
Is a filigree of golden sparks.
With fire-works in their wings
They are transformed, and
Incandescent beings.

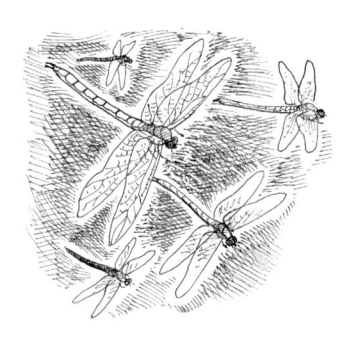

'Kilo-Foxtrot November'

Kilo Foxtrot November was a Piper Cub Special, made of canvas stretched over a light frame and painted white, with green lettering and lines. The little aeroplane had belonged to Denis Zaphiro, Game Warden, and later to Tony Dyer. The year Guy learnt to fly at Wilson airport, he had bought it for £2,000 which he raised by selling a small flat his mother had owned in Nairobi. An aeroplane was much more useful to him than a flat.

KFN seemed to have a character of its own, and it had an influence on our lives almost as great as that of any living thing. It was our magic carpet, but quite without the 'doormat' quality that the word carpet may imply. Inside there was room for two people sitting one behind the other, with a small box behind the back seat for a minimum of baggage – usually extra fuel and emergency supplies; and an empty tin for emergencies of a different sort. It was its smallness and the fact that the wing was above you so that you had an uninterrupted view of the ground, that made flying in KFN such an immediate and direct sensation; quite different from the second-hand flying achieved in anything larger and more powerful. Between you and the airways of eagle and vulture was only a single thickness of woven flax, and the thin perspex of the windows. KFN responded to every bump, updraught, downdraught, head wind, tail wind and cross wind, like a bird. For the pilot, Guy, it must have seemed almost that he himself was this bird, for the aeroplane's responses were largely his responses – of feet on rudder; of hand on ailerons and throttle.

I used often to dream that I was flying solo in KFN and always, it seemed, went through the right motions from take-off to landing so that perhaps, in an emergency, I might actually have been able to fly KFN myself. But the real-life flights behind Guy were so satisfying that I completely lost my previous desire to learn to fly a powered aircraft, although before meeting Guy I had started to learn to glide.

Sometimes when flying low, we would open the window that was almost half the right side of the cabin. Then, the warm smells of the earth below would float in. There was the delicious scent of vegetation as we came over the Uaso Nyiro river, as of hothouses at Kew, which

KFN

must rise as an essence and not linger near the ground. One does not notice it when walking.

Guy said that he could do more ranching in five minutes from the air than he could in a day on the ground. Almost at once it would be apparent where each herd and flock was grazing, and if all was well the herdsmen would hold up both hands. Guy could see which gullies held water, where the grass was best, and if herds of buffalo were near the cattle. Lost animals could often be found within a minute or two of take-off that might have taken all day, or longer, to find on foot. Because the 'plane could fly slowly, reasonably accurate game counts could be done for the whole ranch in a few hours.

During such ranching flights I often felt sick, specially when repeatedly diving to indicate the position of lost cattle to searchers on foot. The 'plane would bank steeply in order to keep the cattle in view, causing the earth to tilt suddenly sideways like a wall beside the window, while on the other side there seemed to be a bottomless void of sky. The ground would enlarge, coming into focus as if seen through a microscope, each stone and bush suddenly distinct as we dived nearer. Then, sickeningly, it would sink away again, leaving one's tummy behind and a tight feeling behind one's eyes, until we were once again high above it – only to repeat the process.

Corrugated iron hangar for KFN

When I was pregnant we would fly to Nairobi for my monthly prenatal checks with the doctor. Then, the dry canvas-smell of the inside of the 'plane made me feel ill even before getting in. It was all I could do to hang on during the hour's bumpy flight southwards over the steeply undulating country of the Kikuyu reserve, between Mt. Kenya and the Aberdares. Upon approaching Wilson airport, Guy would put on his headphones to contact the control tower. If, as sometimes happened, we were told to make a circuit or two above the aerodrome before landing, I would succumb at once, desperately grabbing for the empty tin. Side slipping to lose altitude before finally landing, was awful. Once at a standstill I would stagger thankfully from the 'plane to lie in the shade of the wing on the crisp, golden grass, while Guy chocked the wheels and tied the wings down. Soon, the warm, clean wind blowing from the savannah of Nairobi National Park would revive me.

The longest flight Guy and I made together in KFN was to the Serengeti, flying from Wilson via Lake Natron, a huge fulminating pan of red and white soda; along the Loita hills with their hangers of woodland and buffalo-frequented glades, over the forested rift of Lake Manyara; around the caldera of Ngorogoro, and back to the golden plains of Seronera.

Plains of Seronera

Just after he had learnt to fly, Guy went to Galana, a million-acre ranch on the way to the coast. Owing to headwinds it took him longer to get there than he had expected, and as the sea of bush below was losing distinctness in growing dusk, the engine ran out of fuel and died. As KFN glided with only the rushing of the air outside to be heard, Guy chose an open area of orange earth on which to make an emergency landing. It was the end of the Galana airstrip, and Guy made a perfect landing on it just as the last light faded!

As our family grew it became impossible for us all to fit into KFN. We needed to buy a family vehicle; and the time involved in getting an annual certificate of airworthiness, and Guy's annual medical certificate; the expense of maintenance and aerofuel, the difficulty of getting from Wilson airport into town, finally drove Guy to part with KFN.

It was somehow maiming to lose the power of flight, but there had been times when I had worried. Night falls so fast on the equator with only a short dusk, and more than once I had been about to rush up to the airstrip with hurricane lamps to show Guy where to land: then, at very last light heard the familiar drone of the engine as KFN came safely home. It was too small a 'plane to have the instruments needed for safe night flying.

Anthony Dyer, keen to own KFN once more, bought it. We watched the little aeroplane take off from El Karama taxi-way for the last time – watched until the familiar form was cut off from view

Hurricane lamp

by rising ground beyond the taxi-way; and listened till we could no longer hear the sound of the engine.

Next day at Wilson airport, during welding work on the tail, the canvas bodywork caught fire and KFN was completely destroyed.

But in my mind's eye I can still see Guy swinging the propeller to start the engine, then clambering into his seat: see him signal for the chocks to be removed and after they had been handed in and stowed in the box behind me, see him close the flimsy door and window panels. I can vividly imagine bumping up the taxi-way, so near to the ground, swinging round at the top with an extra boost from the engine to face down the strip, though unable to see directly down it owing to the reared up nose in front of us. Flight checks consisted of testing that door and window were properly shut, seatbelts fastened, flaps and rudder working freely, engine revving. I can feel now the run for take-off, lifting almost at once if there was a head-wind, the 'plane so light you could hardly hold it down; see the strip sliding away to one side beneath as we quickly gained height. I can feel the vibration of, and hear, the engine that was so loud we had to shout to make ourselves heard; can still hear above that noise the spat of rain-drops from the edge of a storm, on the windscreen, and see the long wriggling line made by each as it slanted across the perspex. I can see the mountain ahead becoming whole, like a Japanese wood-block print; and below, the tiny figures of giraffes sloping through the bush.

The mountain made whole

Some Birds

Icarus

A Crowned crane, whom we named Icarus, was found lying under a power cable near Thika, having been electrocuted. Both wings were blasted off at the second joint. Somehow the crane had survived this terrible shock, and when we first saw him he had already been in a small cage at a school for five and a half years. Sharing the cage was a companion crane, Beauty, which had been kidnapped as a youngster, and they spent their restricted lives singing duets, eating maize meal, and watching the children of the school go by. Crane duets consist of deep, resonant single notes, repeated over and over by both birds – an oddly hypnotic and pleasing sound. Now and again wild cranes flew over, the silver notes of their calls dropping down to the captives, who answered. But somehow the call of a grounded crane sounds flat and despairing.

We felt sorry for the cranes while our girls were at the school, and when they left we enquired if we might take the birds home with us. The school was pleased to find them a new home, for it transpired there were plans to destroy Icarus. In his boredom he often over-preened his wing-stubs till they were raw, and they never healed properly. Cranes are said sometimes to go for people's eyes and this was the reason that they had been caged; to prevent possible accidents to the schoolchildren.

The moment the cranes saw us approaching their cage when we came to collect them, they knew something was about to happen to them. They became wildly excited, prancing about and jerking their heads up and down. Yet we had approached them many times before without eliciting this response. They were caught by their attendant and shut in the tarpaulin-covered back of our vehicle, where they began at once to beat frantically against the partition till I thought they might kill themselves. It was only when we started to move, and they had to concentrate on balancing, that they quietened. By the time we reached home that night, over a long distance of rough roads, they must have been exhausted. They were left in the back of the car to recover.

Crowned Crane

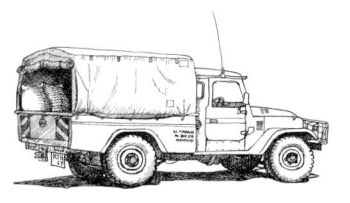

Our Landcruiser

Cranes in vegetable garden

As we did not want to subject the cranes to the shock of being handled again, I built a tunnel of hessian from the back of the vehicle to the open door of the wired-in vegetable garden, where we intended to keep them until they grew used to their new surroundings. They took a long time to pluck up courage to leave the car, and then, to enter the garden. Once inside, the flighted bird took off with velocity and crashed against the overhead chicken wire. He did this over and over again until, his crown battered, he gave up and went to stand facing his old home to the south, weaving to and fro with his breast to the wire.

The cranes stayed in the garden for a few months, until the vegetables were destroyed and Icarus's wing stubs were completely healed. They had enjoyed the novelty of stretching their legs in this new, large enclosure. They had grown used to the dogs passing outside. So now we left their door open. They were free.

We wondered if Beauty would leave immediately; if he would be able to fend for himself in the wild; where he would go; if Icarus would feel bereft when he did go. But the crane stayed with Icarus, though he often made short flights.

There is a high water tank near the vegetable garden, and after about a year Beauty began to stand on the edge of it, apparently enjoying the extensive view to be gained from this vantage. Soon after he had begun to do this, we had to leave home for a few days. Just as we were leaving in the car, I mentioned that we should cover the tank with chicken-wire when we got home, to prevent accidents. Guy said he had had the same thought. But when we returned we were told that the unfortunate crane had already stepped off the side of the tank into the water, and drowned. And this sad occurrence was one of the many illustrations we have had of how important it is to respond to such inner promptings as soon as one has them.

So Icarus stalked the yard, garden and paddocks alone. Often he called. He would stand amongst the poultry for company; and he would gaze at his own reflection in windows, then rest by them for hours as if comforted by the 'other' bird he saw reflected there. Neither of these things had he ever done before.

Crowned cranes

Icarus did not like the cats and once he chased 'Bear' right into the kitchen, and stood amongst us there with his feathers ruffled and cape spread, while the cat fled into the store. But he was frightened of a little Paradise flycatcher which would dive-bomb him on the lawn. He would duck and shy and cower, and eventually beat an undignified retreat to the back yard.

Some months after the loss of Icarus's companion, an emissary of five wild cranes flew in on their great white-panelled wings, and walked with him on the lawn. Their court clothes and finery were so outlandishly beautiful that I felt they needed fanfares of trumpets to announce their coming and going. There was something Elizabethan about their splendour, and for the few days they stayed one seemed to hear music of lute and harpsichord as they turned their heads towards each other in serious, noble conversation; and the garden was as if tented with cloth-of-gold.

One of these cranes stayed when the others left, and Icarus was no longer alone.

The courtship of Icarus and his wild mate was beautiful. They walked slowly side by side, sometimes stopping to stare with their pale blue eyes for long moments into each others faces. At first 'Wild' was afraid of people and dogs, and would fly as soon as one appeared. Icarus would run with her and as she took off make a huge bound, quickly flapping the stubs of his wings. It was as if, just for a second, he had forgotten he could not fly. But as Wild lifted up and away to the freedom of the air, Icarus would land heavily and call after her with his loud, flat voice. Perhaps we felt worse about this than Icarus did himself; who can know what goes on in the mind of a bird?

Icarus led Wild about his old haunts, teaching her that good food was available in the poultry yard and that people and dogs were not quite as dangerous as she thought. Gradually she became tamer. When rain fell and the earth turned soft and green they would spend all day walking together, lured farther and farther by the joys of the Springtime; and by evening were sometimes a mile away, and had to be searched for. Icarus would be shepherded slowly and reluctantly home, to be enclosed in his night boma. Wild would fly in after him at dusk, to roost on the wire netting of his enclosure or on a nearby tree. Sometimes Icarus, who was not one to be trifled with, refused to be shepherded and the patience of the poultry-tender, Liburu, would be tried. One evening we saw this gnome-like little man striding smugly past the kitchen with Icarus tucked firmly under his arm, like the Queen of Spades with a croquet-mallet flamingo. We looked at each other in horror, and had time only to exclaim 'That doesn't look very safe!', when Liburu reappeared, minus crane, to complain that he had been stabbed in the arm.

Icarus mobbed

Crowned cranes

There was a sadness in the courtship of the cranes for Icarus could not balance, without his wings, on Wild's back for mating – though he tried. Even if mating had been possible I do not think Wild would have consented to nest where people and dogs could see her, though they sometimes picked up sticks and tossed them towards each other. We felt Wild wished to lure Icarus to Murera dam, where she often flew herself, in order to nest. But we could not allow that, for Icarus on foot would not survive long in the bush.

Nearly two years passed and in spite of many visits from wild cranes, with whom Wild would fly around the homestead, she always returned to Icarus when they left. But one day a big bird flew in and attacked Icarus repeatedly. While Icarus took refuge in the garden, the white velvet of his cheeks crossed with red weals, 'Kali' ('Fierce') tried hard to win Wild, boldly following her about and feeding with her in the poultry runs. After repeated visits her remarkable loyalty was undermined and Kali stole Wild away. They were missing long enough to breed, and we hoped they did. Wild then returned and spent some months with Icarus, until carried off again by an angry Kali. But they later visited quite often.

While Wild and Kali were away Icarus often called, though he seemed resigned and not at all discontented with his life. If something had happened to Kali and Wild had found herself free once more, I believe she would have returned to Icarus permanently. I expected her to appear any day; and so, I believe, did Icarus. But one morning after he had been with us for five years, we found him lying in his night boma, his beautiful head twisted under him. We thought he might have been bitten by a snake, but we never knew his true age. At the moment he died his remnant wings beat softly on the ground – the long, graceful strokes of true flight – and I thought that Icarus was airborne; completely free at last.

Wild cranes still visit us regularly, but do not stay long now that there is no answer to their calls.

Poultry

'Mook-took' and 'Paley-trotly' were hens belonging to, and named by, Laria and Bella when they were little girls. Mook-took was one of the last Scots Grey Dumpies (a near-extinct domestic breed) on the ranch, speckled black and white with a floppy crown; and Paley-trotly was buff. The girls would spend hours digging up beetle grubs for their hens and the hen's chicks. Murray had a white drake whom he named after a pirate – 'Black Jake'.

The poultry runs are behind the house, their gates always open, except at night, so that the mixed flock of turkeys, hens, bantams

Liburu with crane

Kali and Wild on 'castle' chimney

Beetle grub

and Muscovy ducks can run free in the farmyard. They are an important part of our self-sufficiency as there are nearly always plenty of eggs, and meat whenever it is needed. Nearly all the pillows and cushions in the house and at our visitors' bandas are stuffed with feathers which are saved, sorted and washed. This is a lengthy and sneeze-provoking job which I usually do in the bathroom – and each time vow never to bother with again.

We were often told that keeping mixed poultry 'free range' was uneconomical. So Laria, with the aid of her school calculator, did some sums and discovered that, in our case, this was not true. However, we used to have a flock of geese, which we could not bring ourselves to eat. They were not very successful at breeding, seldom hatching more than one or two green and yellow downy goslings at a time. Perhaps this was because of the usual lack of green grass. In one bad drought it became impossible to buy any food for the geese, so we packed the whole flock into the cage of the pick-up and drove them, anxiously standing upright on their orange paddles, up the slopes of the mountain to a dam at a friend's house where there would always be green grass and pond weed. I missed their calls, so like those of wild greylags in Autumn, in Scotland.

Old house in hen run

Geese

Apart from geese, the chickens and bantams are the least productive of the poultry but we keep them so as not to have, literally, all our eggs in one basket; and the cocks are valued for their beauty. Their crowing acts as a night clock for they are exceptionally punctual, starting at three thirty a.m. They are also a kind of animated weather vane, for if the cocks crow during rain we can expect that the shower will not last long and the weather will clear up. They seem never to be wrong in this respect. But if they stand with their tails slanting right down it will soon rain hard, and if the ducks point their beaks skywards, wriggling their heads from side to side, rain is usually not far off, though occasionally they are mistaken. Once, in a downpour which transformed the yard into lakes and rivers almost instantly, I found a broody hen in her nest-box trying to sit on a clutch of eggs which were floating around her in four inches of water. Diverting the flood and giving her fresh bedding, we

'It will soon rain'

SOME BIRDS 93

reinstalled her upon the eggs and the whole clutch hatched successfully the next day. Hens can certainly be brave. One day when I was visiting the old house at Combretum, I saw a hen attack an eagle. She belonged to a herdsman who was spending the nights at the house to keep an eye on it for us. This hen and her family of recently hatched chicks was foraging in the open, when I heard an odd tearing sound in the air followed by a loud whistle. A tawny eagle had stooped on the family, and now stood on the ground with a chick clasped in one foot. The hen, ruffled to twice her normal very small size, flung herself against the breast of the eagle over and over again, screeching in fury. As I ran towards them the eagle flew to a nearby tree, still clutching the unfortunate chick. The other chicks, flattened to the ground, remained invisible until the hen gave the 'all clear' after the eagle had gone. Then up they sprang and legged it to her as fast as they were able. The herdsmen often keep chickens at the bomas, and such a hen, the only one at her particular boma, had already raised to half size her whole brood of ten scrawny chicks. Left outside all alone during the day when the cattle and herdsmen were absent, she had managed to outwit hawks, eagles, mongooses, jackals and snakes without losing a single chick. When I saw them they had no water: offered a dish of it they drank, but perfunctorily, for they were truly Spartan chickens. Their survival cannot be put down to luck alone, for eagles pass over every day. It seems chickens, like other birds, can learn through experience.

Hen house at heifer boma

Our turkeys, gangling and noisy, look much like wild turkeys in the woods of North America. Most are the traditional bronze and have the racehorse build of the wild bird and the same savoury meat; quite unlike the bulging, cotton-wool-tasting commercial breed. We bought our first stock from a roadside village where, presumably through natural selection, this wilder type had come to predominate. Turkeys thrive here and if left to breed unchecked would soon over-run us. All day the gobblers strut and fan, shooting forwards smoothly as if on wheels, blushing red or blue, scraping their wings along the ground and booming in their chests. The gobbling parties when many birds gobble together, usually in response to some extraneous sound, are so loud you cannot hear yourself, or anyone else, speak.

Turkeys

We had twenty-two homing pigeons in the back yard. One morning all but a grey cock bird were lying dead, heaped on the bottom shelf of the dovecote. A black-tipped mongoose had made use of the step-ladder which had been left accidentally in front of the dovecote, to climb up. It had entered through a small hole in the wire netting of the door and killed each pigeon with a single bite on the back of the head, but it had been unable to pull the birds out of the hole as they were too fat. There was no sign of the grey cock bird.

Two months later I saw what we thought was the twenty-second pigeon, the grey cock (who must have been thinner than the others and escaped through the hole) feeding with wild ring-necked doves and speckled pigeons at the home of distant neighbours. Soon, those neighbours acquired homing pigeons of their own with which our bird then lived. Our dovecote was re-stocked from theirs, as we missed the soothing bubble of pigeon voices and the cote, empty and silent for a year, seemed a reproach. Their numbers are kept in check, at around twenty, by Tiger, one of Ndimu's wild cat 'kittens' – now a magnificent but unruly feline.

Ranch Dovecote

Platypus

Muscovy ducks, domesticated during the ancient civilisations of Central America, do well in this dry land unsuited, one would have thought, to ducks. They stump about the farm yard and appear unexpectedly, and somehow incongruously, in every nook of the garden and even occasionally on the roof and chimneys. There is a small concrete pond behind the dairy in which they swim and float happily, ducking themselves and preening their feathers. In spite of this the drakes appear especially disreputable, for not only are their faces covered with red and black protrusions, but their feathers are often dishevelled from fighting. The ducks produce large and beautiful families of fluffy yellow and black ducklings, and sometimes we have to look after weaklings and late hatchers at the house until they are strong enough to rejoin their families. Platypus was such a duckling.

Her round head was as of brown velvet, her eyes grey, and her beak shiny brown with a pink lower mandible. Below the silvery down of her throat her breast was dusky yellow; but the rest of her was sooty black. Her legs and paddles were like black patent leather except for two small triangular panels of yellow between the toes of each foot. She had been the only duckling to be hatched from a clutch the ownership of which had been disputed by three ducks, and as a result the eggs had not been properly brooded by any of them. There seemed to be something wrong with her legs, for they stuck out to the sides, which caused her to walk with an exaggeratedly rolling gait like a tiny drunken sailor. Platypus refused at once to be left alone, even in the comfort of a softly lined box on a hot water bottle. She had to come with us wherever we went, in a padded sponge bag hung round the neck. Now and again she would force open the Velcro which closed the bag, with the top of her head, to survey her surroundings with bright, intelligent eyes; standing on tiptoes in the corner of the bag like a small, elongated and furry pear.

Black-tipped mongoose

Bantam cocks foretelling

SOME BIRDS

Platypus

Theophilus inspecting waste-paper basket

At night we would settle Platypus in a box with her hot water bottle, beside the bed. But she cheeped and called incessantly. I tried putting my hand inside the box so that she could sit on it, but that was never good enough. She wanted to be in the bed! As soon as I put her on the sheet she would run full tilt to push between my neck and the pillow, shoving herself in firmly with her little paddles, and making small, satisfied chirrups. Every so often she would nibble my neck to remind me she was still there; as if the soft humidity of her powder-puff body were not enough. One slept only fitfully for fear of squashing her, so Bella and I took two-hourly stints with Platypus through the nights. And she always tucked herself under our necks, hardly having the patience to wait until we were comfortably settled.

For the first two days Platypus had been almost too weak to stand, but she gained strength quickly and could soon run at great speed, her feet pattering so fast they were almost a blur beneath her. But as soon as she left the cloths we put down for her, her legs would shoot outwards on the slippery floor and she would then move like a skater, pushing herself along from side to side. If we left the room for a few minutes, Platypus would run to greet us upon our return with welcoming chirrups, as if we had been away for a week. All day she made contact trills and would often nibble our hands, faces or necks with that affectionate preening motion. At regular intervals she would come for brooding, when she climbed inside one's shirt or jersey to sleep for a quarter of an hour. In fact, she became a full time job for the two of us.

Platypus was fed on duckling mash but she much preferred the flies we killed for her with a fly swatter. Every time she heard a bang (or any other loud noise) she would hurry over and crane up at our towering bulk, brightly alert to receive the expected fly. She had no fear of other animals. When Vortrix, a big dog, bent down with avuncular expression to sniff her, she pecked him on the nose. Likewise Theophilus Warren, a fierce buck rabbit, when he came up to investigate. Her friendly confidence and the way she waggled her tail so jauntily was endearing to everyone who saw her, and although all ducklings are sweet of course, we felt that Platypus had an unusual quota of personality.

Soon she was strong enough to spend some time with a family of larger ducklings in the chicken run. The mother duck was still brooding them but not as often as Platypus required, so we would collect her for extra brooding and feeding. At this time she became rather smelly and acquired the name 'Reeky-beaky'. Because of this it was a relief to be able to hand her over to the care of the mother duck at night; and we were badly short of sleep.

Platypus's beak became steadily larger but the rest of her did not seem to keep up in proportion to it. One day, we noticed that she was again rolling in her gait and seemed a bit tired. The next morning after breakfast, Bella went as usual to collect her from the duck house but came hurrying in again to ask where she was. Going out together we found her small corpse on the roof of the house where it had been placed by Liburu, the poultry man, who had discovered her dead when he had looked in on the family earlier. We think that the other ducklings, being so much larger than Platypus, had inadvertently smothered her during the night.

Though Platypus lived little more than three weeks, the affection she had inspired and the amusement she had given us was out of all proportion to her size.

❋

Not long ago a female leopard had been seen in broad daylight, standing at the kennels looking in at the dogs. Murray had chased her off into the River Paddock with the vehicle he was passing in at the time. A few nights later a leopard took a goat out of the stables, jumping in, and out with the goat, over the half door. After that we fixed a grid over the top half of the door. A boy cutting wood near a small house known as The Cottage, at about 9 o'clock one morning, saw a leopard very close, staring at him. He stopped wood-cutting and left in a hurry. He had not liked the way the leopard was looking at him.

Then, just after we had gone to bed one night, the watchman rang the gate bell (an old goat-bell hung in the hedge). There was a leopard in the turkey run, he said. We went out. There she was, crouched in the middle of the run beside a dead turkey, almost invisible in her spots, while turkeys and chickens cackled and flapped on their perches. Suddenly the leopard began to ricochet around the run, bouncing off the mesh walls. I opened the door so that she could get out, but she seemed unable to remember how she had entered (through a smallish gap in the corner of the mesh roof). We withdrew, hoping she would find the open door and run off. But a while later she was still there. An old red cock suddenly lost his nerve and began to run up and down, tottering and screaming. Guy decided he should shoot the leopard as he felt sure she was the one that had been frequenting the back yard. If released she would obviously be a danger to the dogs, and possibly to children if, as it seemed, she was unable to hunt in the wild. After he had shot her we found her canine teeth were broken and worn to stubs. She was much larger than she appeared to be in the light of the torch when alive, but thin. The turkeys, some of whom had escaped from the enclosure after I opened the door, were dotted about the back yard frozen like statues, their heads stretched out in front of them. They did not react when touched, so we picked them up one at a time and returned them to the run, where they remained in the same positions,

Turkey on garden gate

rigid with shock! The ducks and chickens which had run off to the garages, or flown into trees, we left outside.

It was interesting, we thought, that the leopard had refrained from striking out wildly at the rest of the poultry after killing the chosen turkey, but that would seem to be in line with the quiet methods used by cats. It puzzled us that she did not leave the way she had entered, when surprised by the night-watchman; or by the door after it had been opened.

Branding fire with heating irons

DROUGHT

Where is rain? Where
Do wet clouds warp the sky
While under them gauze curtains close the hills?

The light is harsh; here
The bare overhead cannot cry.
Below, dead and sere, the land with dust fills.

Herds in lethargy move, thinned.
Grass is sticks, grey and charred,
It pricks and trips dull, stumbling hooves.

No quenching spatter exhilarates this wind –
It drives sheets of dust through the yard
And bangs the corrugated rooves.

Fire and Drought, Rain and River

We had seen the smoke in the afternoon and thought the fire not very big, and that it would probably be put out quite quickly. But after dark we realised that it was huge. A line of terrific flames lay along the horizon and every now and again spurting torches of white heat erupted, like flares on the surface of the sun, as a tree or bush was consumed. The smoke from the fire was like a round, molten mountain, as it reflected the light of the flames hundreds of feet into the air. Above the flames it was brilliant orange and red, and higher, a feverish scarlet. Finally it became lavender against the blue-black of the night sky. Upon this furnace-like background, the hangar across the river showed up angular, and the houses and huts of our labour lines were silhouetted black. Behind us, in strange and beautiful contrast, the moon sailed serenely in dapples of silver cloud, cool and mild.

It would have been impossible for anyone, then, to approach that fire nearer than two hundred yards, so Guy decided to take men to help fight it very early in the morning when the wind would have dropped. But in the morning the fire was already out, except for smouldering wrecks of the larger trees in the black and smoking sea of ash. And the fire was not, as we had thought, just across the river on the neighbouring ranch, but miles away on quite a different

Wet sack and leafy branch for fighting fire

Fighting a fire (Guy on right) 1999

property. A burn-back had been lighted in the path of the seemingly invincible conflagration and it had died: hoist with its own petard.

Although intelligence overcame the fire, carelessness had started it. Honey hunters had used a bunch of smouldering grass to smoke bees, then left it lying on the ground to wreak its havoc. Many bush fires are started in this way.

In dry seasons we often see great fires on the moorlands of Mt. Kenya and the Aberdares, which glare sullenly at night like red-hot lava floes on the flanks of volcanoes, and the atmosphere is tanged with tawny smoke for weeks on end. Sometimes smoke causes the sun to shine with a strange orange light which casts only weak shadows on the ground. After the fires are out, ash whirls dervishly on the wind like ghosts of the burnt land.

Dust devils

Drought is a trouble we have had to face more often than fire, and it has longer lasting and farther reaching effects. The dread of drought is never completely out of mind, even in times of green plenty. It circles like the shadow of a starved wolf, receding at times, but always ready to return. Sometimes it appears in fact, no longer a shadow, and we must face it. I have come to hate it more than anything, for the suffering it brings and for its dreariness.

In 1981 no rain had fallen in the short November rains, so that by the time the main rains should have arrived in April or May of 1982, the bush was already seriously droughted. The signs that usually precede the rains, that year gave a strange mixture of signals. Some blossom was unusually scanty, but the whistling thorn flowered as few people had seen before. The whole countryside was one great orchard of thick, creamy, scented blossom. Many thought that this meant there would be wonderful rain, but one very old Maasai said that, when the thorn trees blossomed like this it meant a terrible drought. He was right. The weeks after the rains should have begun lengthened into months, and animals and plants lost hope and began to die. Hat-rack zebras wandered aimlessly over the bare ground and warthogs, having no longer the energy to find and dig up roots, died in great numbers. Along the roads of Laikipia and elsewhere, dying cattle lay abandoned; and the carcases of thousands of others were left to rot or mummify. Their bones and skulls were later gathered into cairns.

To begin with we brought in expensive lorry-loads of feed for the cattle, but soon there was no more available owing to the widespread nature of the drought and its unusual length. So we gathered leaves of mukinyea (*Euclea divinorum*), a more or less evergreen shrub, and the bark of trees that had been pushed down by elephants, and even the bark from gum poles, and ground these ingredients together in the posho mill to make a meal of some nutritional value and bulk. It was mixed with cotton-seed husk and the chopped pads

Piece of Prickly-pear eaten by baboons

FIRE AND DROUGHT, RAIN AND RIVER

of prickly pear, blow-lamped to remove the spines. This food and roughage was spread at each boma on long strips of hessian held down by poles, and sprinkled with molasses. When the exhausted cattle shuffled in through clouds of dust after their long walk to the river to drink, and a day of almost fruitless foraging, they ate this strictly rationed mixture with desperate appreciation.

The weakest cattle, hardly more than skeletons held together by skin, were brought to the house. It was exhausting and often discouraging work for the men, lifting those too weak to stand, three times every day. These cattle developed large sores from inactivity and malnutrition and though some eventually recovered, others died or had to be destroyed.

Cows recovering from drought in the garden 1974

Meanwhile, blinding sheets of dust were driven through the back yard by a bleak wind that banged the corrugated iron roof and rolled chicken feathers into scruffy drifts. The light from the setting sun reflected first in pale pink bars radiating across the dust-laden atmosphere, and later as an angry gash of fiery orange along the horizon. Nights were very cold. Vultures, hyaenas and jackals were the only creatures with enough to eat – but even they suffered, as starved meat holds little nourishment.

No one who has not experienced such a drought can know the exhilaration of feeling the first spots of rain on the wind, nor the arrow of joy that shoots through one's heart at the sight of the first blotting of the horizon with falling rain. But for the starving animals, the longed-for rain is often the coup-de-grace, for they cannot stand the extra stress of being cold and wet, and their exhausted systems cannot cope with the first shoots of new green grass.

We see Grévy's zebras on the ranch all year round, and White-browed sparrow-weavers breed increasingly along the river, spreading upstream, their calls evocative of the low, drier country to the North. Occasionally there are small parties of Vulturine guinea fowls, and

Weathered giraffe skull

sometimes even gerenuks. The appearance of these creatures, which were not here when we first came, may indicate a gradual change to a more desert climate; though after rain that is difficult to believe, for then the silky sea of grasses is three feet deep and stretches, alive with flowers and butterflies, as far as you can see. At the same time, with a general increase in wild life on the ranch, the number of cows that can be supported has gone down from a beast to ten acres, twenty years ago, to a beast to twenty acres today; so that it cannot support more than seven hundred to eight hundred cattle (not counting calves at foot). There have always been patches of ground too hard and smooth for rain to soak into, which we work to reclaim by spreading manure from the bomas in lines along the contours. This holds up rainwater and seeds, allowing plants to take root and grow which would not otherwise be able to do so. It is an effective measure but takes time and labour as the manure is moved by ox-cart and donkey cart and spread with shovels.

Recently, settlement, subsistence farming and over-grazing have spread in Laikipia, bringing with them poverty and hunger. South of El Karama there was thick bush and grassland through which elephants and all the other wild creatures wandered, and cattle grazed productively. But in 1990 settlers who had been evicted from a forest reserve began to move to the land against our boundary. They lit fires to burn off trees and shrubs, and many times we sent all available hands to prevent fires that had got out of control from

White-browed sparrow-weavers

Grévy's zebra

Manure on the contours

coming Northwards. From the airstrip the land to the South looked scorched and brown, and the first huts began to go up, their corrugated iron twinkling in the sun. One evening a few months later, we walked to the gate on our Southern boundary. It was as if a malevolent fairy had waved a wand. The bush had gone! A bare vista stretched on either side of a dusty track, which was dotted with receding figures. A few men dug irresolutely outside their shanties; drooping stalks of prematurely dried-up maize rattled in the wind.

After four years many of the smallholders had been on famine relief since they arrived, because there is seldom enough rain to produce proper harvests and wild animals eat what little harvest there is. Though some of the settlers have since moved away again, others have come, and school and clinic have been built with local effort and aid, so that many people have become entrenched on this land, climatically unsuited, it would seem, to agriculture.

Compared to the priceless blessing of the rain the troubles it may bring are insignificant. However, in a heavy storm, so much rain may fall so quickly that at once the ground is awash with hurrying sheets of water, and gullies are suddenly cafe-au-lait torrents which whirl away drought-bared soil, and sometimes drown impalas. The main gullies can become swirling rivers and where they cross tracks, lakes spread which are sometimes too deep to drive through, and more than twice have had to be swum: by the men and horses on patrol, and by a visiting cousin caught out in a storm. A number of times we have spent the night in the car or stayed with neighbours if they could be reached, when we were unable to get home.

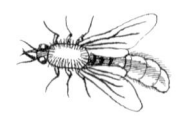

Ranch dams fill and the water flows out of their spillways like smooth gushes of oil, wrinkled where they touch the ends of the dam walls, swollen and sullenly roaring as they plunge along the gullies below. The dam walls are sometimes breached with house-sized holes and it is a major work to rebuild them. Once, a drift below our largest dam, Murera, was transformed overnight into an eight foot trench, twenty feet wide. We replaced it with another drift, 30 yards across, above the dam. This we built from concrete reinforced with wire and scrap metal collected over time, including ancient wheelbarrows, so that one day the drift might be a source of interesting

Murera drift

agricultural 'fossils'. Sometimes there is too much water flowing down the gully to allow a vehicle or someone wading, to cross the drift, and quite often the headlights have been immersed as our old diesel Landcruiser almost swims across, plunging us not only into

"Quagga" with her foal 1981 ♂

Donkey + Common Zebra?
♀
Jan '76.

Ordinary Jackass.

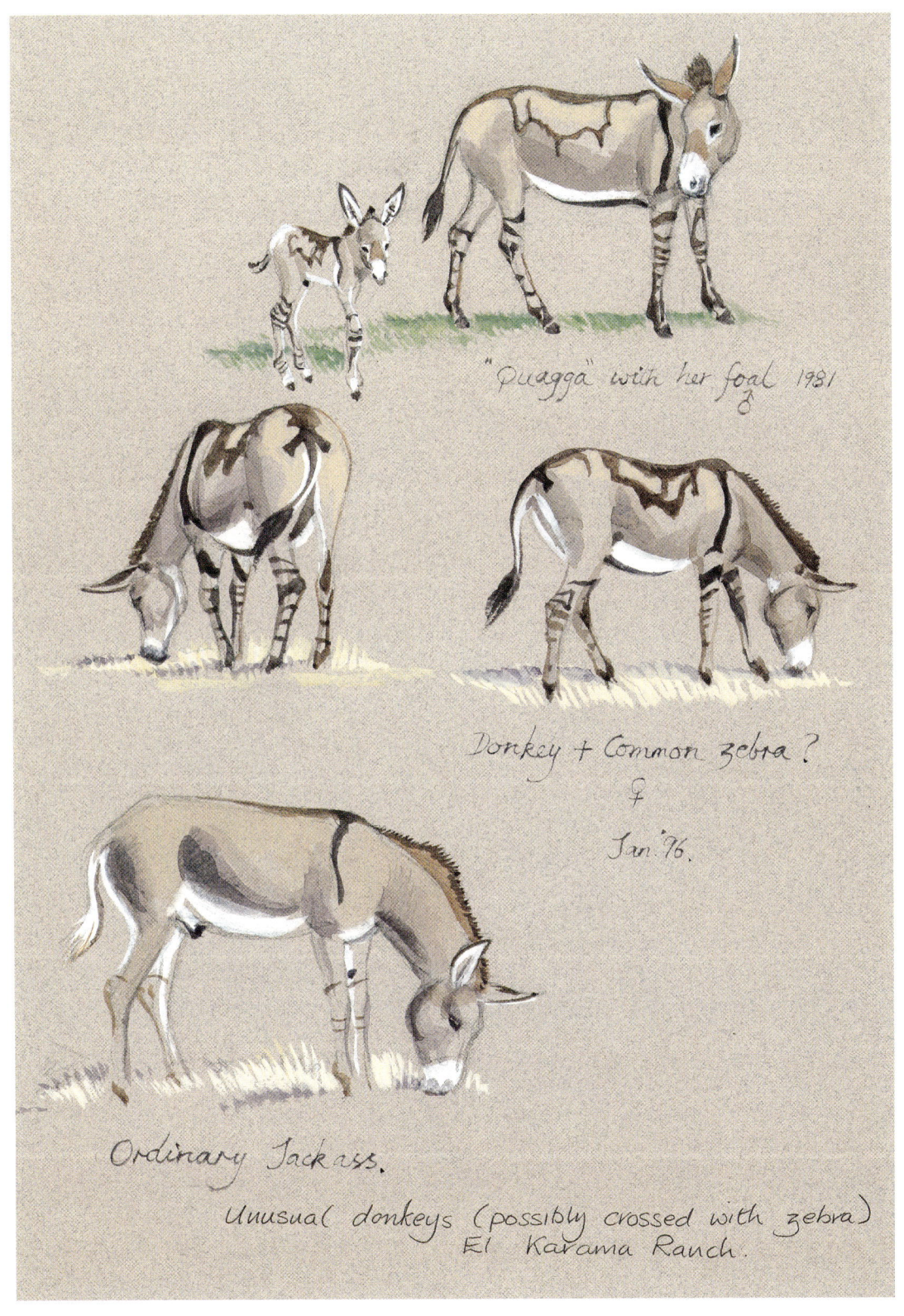

Unusual donkeys (possibly crossed with zebra)
El Karama Ranch.

Unusual donkeys (top and centre) with ordinary Jackass (below) for comparison

Bobby and Nangi

Work at the Hoggit boma, Dec.96

Camels coming home to their boma

Looking upstream from "Fishing Rock", with Red-headed Weaver's nests and patterns made on the water by whiligig beetles. Afternoon.

Upstream from The Fishing Rock

Capparidaceae.   *Capparis tomentosa*

May 92.

Nat. size

Wonderfully scented.

March 92

Prickly shrub, felty leaves. Often scrambling up trees or over other shrubs.

Browsed by eland, poisonous to camels and cattle. Fruit also poisonous.

NSG

Capparis tomentosa

The rock pan at Combretum in the rains looking east towards Mt. Kenya

The rock pan in the rains looking west towards the Aberdares

The falls at Combretum in spate

Combretum bridge flooded

A banda at the river

TERMITES

To murmur of hurrying water busy on the ground,
Winged termites rise: brown snowflakes falling upwards in the sky;
Snowstorms reversed.
Rainwater, to our drought-stricken ears, makes a merry sound,
And with the termites departing, seems all cares die:
In thin air dispersed.

To termites, the trilling of the rain beats a drum to fly;
To quit their crescent doorways in the ochre mud
For freedom of the air.
Tiny workers seeth by entrances to bid good-bye,
Before another drum-roll hits the ground and changing it to flood,
Turns their joy to despair.

The ransom of the rain wreaks fairy magic on the ground,
Returning swelling seeds, exploding buds, for former dirth:
Fecund regeneration.
There, suddenly, where all was bare, flowers and grass abound;
And new ant-hills burgeon bulbous through the earth:
Hardship's exoneration.

the water but into the dark, so we have to guess at the path between the concrete posts on either side of the drift. Occasionally a dam is lost for good when a spillway is eaten back too far by floods, and all the water flows away to leave an empty basin where there should have been a reservoir for the dry weather.

Heavy rain washes silt into the dams too, which, when they dry out later in the year, needs to be removed with the aid of our 36-year-old tractor. Sometimes the oxen are used, though scooping a

Dam-scooping with oxen (Atheru at scoop)

Ox-drawn dam-scoop

dam with oxen seems rather like digging a well with a tea cup. But there is something satisfyingly beautiful in the rhythmical slowness of the oxen and in the hypnotically repeated pattern of their path across the dam, circling to one side, onto the wall where the earth is tipped out, down the far side, round and across the dam once more. The work is done in silence except for an occasional called command, cracked whip, the click of the hooves of the oxen and the 'scrumbling' sound of the dry mud pushed along before the scoop.

There are fifty or more miles of ranch tracks that have to be maintained, with long, curved, cut-off ditches to be kept open on all the slopes to prevent the tracks washing away in the rains. There are sections on thick, black-cotton soil (a heavy volcanic clay) that have to be overlain with red murram, which is dug on the ranch itself, and with stones, if the tracks here are to be passable in the wet weather. After rains the rutted stretches must be graded by the tractor pulling the hand operated grader blade, before the ground dries out and becomes iron hard.

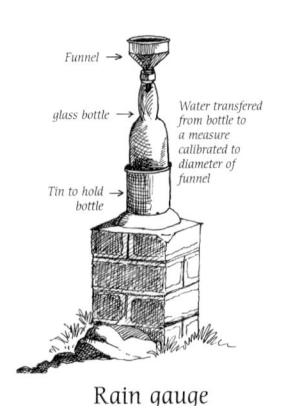

Fordson Power Major

Annual rainfall for El Karama over 50 years has varied from 15.71 inches in a drought to 47.72 inches in a year of flood, but averages 27.73 inches. This may sound quite a lot, but in heat and wind, evaporation is very rapid.

Because rain is so welcome and often long awaited, we enjoy watching how the big drops falling on puddle or river, raise oval bubbles like fishermen's plastic floats which, as soon as they have burst are replaced with others; all jumping joyfully out of the water as if leaping to greet the rain. Or how the first drops to fall are dark

Rain gauge

Funnel →
glass bottle →
Tin to hold bottle →
Water transferred from bottle to a measure calibrated to diameter of funnel

on the ground, and gradually there are so many that the whole earth is dark. Then the wetness glistens and finally water begins to trickle. The thirsty ground drinks it in, then breathes out gently: that wonderful scent of wet earth.

Occasionally there are hail storms that clatter deafeningly on the iron rooves. Afterwards, the hailstones lie in drifts of icy slush on the ground. The children used to gather this in buckets for it was the nearest thing to snow on El Karama, though we often see new snow powdered far down the shoulders of the Mountain. Only one frost has been recorded on the ranch, which caused the trees in the gullies to turn brown and lose their leaves.

Sometimes rain falls softly with a tinkling purr on the water of the house dam, and perhaps a pair of Crowned cranes will be there to add their melancholy music. On the trees, lichens, formerly so dry and grey, take up moisture and in places become an almost phosphorescent lime green, shining in the gloom of a cloudy evening. On the ground, black ants send lone scouts hurrying, or impis of soldiers on their raids. Tracks, which were blurred in the sands of drier weather, now show up clear on the dampened earth. Minty fumes hang on the air where giraffes have passed; and a party of fairy umbrellas may have opened – silvery-mauve toadstools of the utmost delicacy – upon an elephant dropping.

Or a storm may come fast and dark from the East, the javelins of rain like scratches on steel against the melting clouds. It is then that one feels sorry for baby animals, kids and calves, struggling insects and chicks, and for the herdsmen who may not seek shelter till the evening when they return with the stock, damp and cold, to the bomas and to their corrugated-iron huts. But how good their fires and tea must seem then!

The Ewe-goats normally give birth just after the rains, and if these rains were normal, the ewes enjoy the green grass and bushes and produce plenty of milk for their kids. However, in very wet years, when the ground never dries out, sickness can strike the kids. Calves also sometimes suffer in periods of continuous wet and cold, contracting diarrhoea and pneumonia. Bomas must be moved often, or cattle will soon be standing knee deep in mud all night.

When all the land is green, the wild animals quite quickly mow the grass, keeping it short and sweet. I believe this is an advantage to cattle, for the grass never grows into the tangled, unpalatable (to cattle) and woody thickets which, on land with few wild animals (especially zebra) sometimes needs to be burnt: a hazardous undertaking in itself. And it seems that the longer the grass, the more disease there is, even with fewer wild animals, perhaps because more ticks breed in long grass.

The Uaso Nyiro river can rise ten feet or more in a short time and

Rain bubbles

Aard-Vark tracks

Fairy umbrellas

Shade for kids

Baboon

Fresh-water crab

Vervet monkey

sometimes flows over our bridge to Combretum, which is fifteen feet high – recently the river rose 30 feet and swept the bridge away. Then, trees stand knee deep in the almost silent, rushing water which is suddenly full of powerful self-importance. Concentrated utterly on its own being the river coils, a terra-cotta-coloured dragon, through the land. Sometimes the banks are melted away around the roots of trees, so that they crash, forming bridges for leopard and baboon.

At other times, where it flows shallow, the river is refreshing and playful, fanning coolness into the air around as it chuckles over pebbles and rocks; or it is a silent, still presence in the deep stretches below steep green banks and dusky clumps of pink or white-flowered Dombeya. Over it reach the lithe branches of the Yellow-thorns; highways, banqueting halls, cathedrals and dormitories for Vervet monkeys and baboons.

While sitting by the river one afternoon I thought regretfully, 'One day it will go on here without me to admire it'. Then I thought: the river has been there for long ages, and the water creatures and the land creatures have lived in it and by it during their often very brief lives, and been refreshed by it. The world stays here for us, the visitors. The river's banks which seem so permanent with their green covering, are merely harbourage for the trees and plants on their visits. All are visiting, and the river is there for our joy or our drowning. But even the river, which seems so permanent, may be dried up one day by man's need and greed, or by weather changes. So, because I feel that the river too is merely visiting, it seems to me to be a fellow being, however much my intellect tells me it is not alive. And we all, animals and people of El Karama and elsewhere along its course, depend on the river for our living. Without it we would not be here for there is no other permanent source of water.

There is an engine and pump which send river water during

day-time to a tank above the farmyard. In this tank there has always lived a pure race of the fish Tilapia nigra, now a rarity in Kenya due to cross breeding (intentional and unintentional) with other Tilapia species. They remain small owing to limited space and food in the tank. On occasions when the pump has broken down and the water level in the tank has got too low, we have had to rescue the fishes, moving them in buckets to a long trough in the back yard; later

Tilapia nigra

Pump at river, before pump house was built

re-catching them and returning them when the pump is back in action. From this tank the water is fed by gravity to dip, troughs, orchard and houses. Before Guy came there were two weirs built across the river, and a waterwheel and windmill sent water to the homestead. But battering-ram tree trunks carried on the spates made short work of the weirs. The river banks are too high and the fall of the river not abrupt enough to allow a ram to be installed. One day we hope to build underground tanks in which to store water taken from the river when it is in spate, and rainwater from all the rooves of the homestead; for nowadays in dry weather the river is sometimes dangerously low. It is wrong, then, to irrigate from it, for farther downstream, men and animals must dig holes in the sand of the river bed to reach the precious water.

Secretary bird drinking

Guinea fowls in flight

FIRE AND DROUGHT, RAIN AND RIVER

BUFFALO BULLS

Three bulls trot, heavily light,
Into the golden dust of evening,
The sinking sun flashing on their horns
As it filters through the branches
Of blossom-heavy thorns.
We had come upon them unexpected,
Standing to stare, arresting
The mastication of their jaws
In order to hear.
The wind had been wrong,
And after an angry toss
They had gone.

Chirpie

The story of Cheepie the Speke's weaver, whom we raised and returned to the wild, is told in 'Nyamuluki'. But perhaps that of her successor is different enough to be worth relating also. We found Chirpie during the rains, when Speke's weavers breed, inside one of a number of nests that had blown from a tree onto the roof in a strong wind. My heart sank when she was found crouched there, for by then we knew just what hard work it would be to raise her: and I knew we had to try.

We put her on cotton-wool in a box to begin with, because her down and feathers were alive with mites. The mites came off onto the cotton-wool, and after three or four changes of bedding she was more or less free of them. By then she was feeding with gusto for she had opened her beak almost at once, without the initial forcing that had been necessary with Cheepie. Her voice, too, was different from Cheepie's, being deeper and fruitier; and she used it continuously and strongly every time we appeared in her room. After a few days Chirpie could fly from her table to my face or head. It is disconcerting to have a small bird flying at your face and trying to land, with scratchy feet, on your nose or lips. If she perched on my head I had to persuade her to walk from there to a finger in order to feed her. Very soon Chirpie began to help herself to food I left in the room – a thing that Cheepie did only when full-grown. A hard-boiled egg-yolk disappeared and once, upon returning to the room after an absence of a few minutes, I found her looking rather heavy and, I thought (anthropomorphically), slightly guilty, beside an empty saucer that had contained a large amount of finely chopped raw meat. One morning she was surrounded by a drift of moth's wings, all that was left of what I imagined would be half a day's supply of food for her – moths caught by lamplight the previous evening. Where food was concerned she seemed to be a bottomless pit, and soon history was repeating itself in frequent hunts for insects in the paddocks around the house, starting early in the morning when the long grass was heavy with dew and insects comatose after the chill of the night. The sky would be still rosy with dawn, and there was an indescribable freshness to the world. It seemed almost sacrilege to

Laria with Cheepie

Speke's weavers at nest

make darker green tracks through the diamond-and-pearl-encrusted grasses as I walked through them, my skirt quickly soaked and clinging round my legs; Chirpie sitting on my hand and chirping the while. Flocks of Grey-headed social weavers and other Speke's weavers were also searching for breakfast for their chicks, whirring busily to and from their nests. As the sun slowly warmed the pristine world, grasshoppers, crickets and caterpillars began to move about in the grass forest round my feet, and it became easier to see and catch them.

Chirpie swallowing a large cricket

Grey-headed social-weavers nest

Without tuition, Chirpie developed a technique with caterpillars which Cheepie never learnt while she was with us – and this was just one instance of the many differences between them. I expect that Cheepie would have learnt it too if we had known about it and shown her, for I have since noticed that many birds treat caterpillars this way. Taking it by the head and squashing it, Chirpie would pass its body deftly through her beak till she had it by the tail end. Then she beat the caterpillar this way and that against a perch – often our hands – until the stomach contents came out; a green, slimy sausage. After this the caterpillar, now much reduced in bulk, was gathered and given a good chew before being swallowed. If the inside did not come out at once she would return it through her beak until she had the head again, and tweak it off before resuming the beating. All this was quite hard work, and unless she was really hungry she did not bother to eat any but the smallest caterpillars, which were swallowed without treatment in one gulp. She did not like butterflies, lacewings and antlions, and soon refused meat. She enjoyed brown bread; and in these things she also differed from Cheepie.

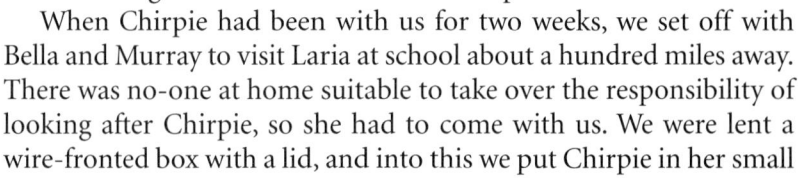

Courting termites

When Chirpie had been with us for two weeks, we set off with Bella and Murray to visit Laria at school about a hundred miles away. There was no-one at home suitable to take over the responsibility of looking after Chirpie, so she had to come with us. We were lent a wire-fronted box with a lid, and into this we put Chirpie in her small nest-basket. At intervals during the rough journey, but without stopping, we would shut the car windows and let her out of her box for feeding. The instant the lid was lifted she popped up through it like a jack-in-the-box. Otherwise she balanced on top of her basket inside the box. Sometimes her chin would bump down onto the basket or, alternately, her legs would be stretched to their limit, as she adjusted herself to the bumps in the road. And always she faced the way we were going.

We stayed that night with friends at Rongai, in the Rift Valley, and next morning, after I had gone on an early insect hunt, I foolishly let Chirpie out into the garden, strange to her, for fresh air and exercise. I had forgotten the small terrier, Kimmy, who took upon himself the job of chasing out of the guava tree, birds which came to eat the fruit. Very useful he was: but the instant Chirpie let out her fruity cheep from that tree, Kimmy came tearing across the garden barking furiously. Chirpie flew to the top of a Pepper tree and stayed there, even after Kimmy had been shut in the house. I had breakfast under the tree hoping she would come down to me. When it was nearly time for us to set out for the school, a Grey-headed shrike dive-bombed her and the two of them flew into the distance, Chirpie a tiny brown dot in the lead. I called and searched for half an hour in the direction she had gone, after which we sadly gave her up for lost. As we went to the car I gave one last call. There was an answer! Chirpie swept over us to the Pepper tree and, to my joy and relief, she came from there to my hand at once. We bundled her unceremoniously into her basket, and Laria was pleased to meet her when we arrived at the school only a few minutes late.

On our way home after this visit there was very heavy rain and the main road was as muddy and slippery as a ploughed field, its deep ruts filled with water. We had to drive slowly but keep moving, or we would have stuck. In the car we had two women who were coming to work for us. Their mattresses, bedding and bags were stuffed in beside them and Bella on the back seat. I held Chirpie's box on my knee, and Murray, who was about five years old at the time, sat beside me on the front seat. In the dark, one puddle seemed endless, and suddenly we saw that the water ahead was flowing across the road. 'Look out Guy – it's a river!' – and so it was. There was a terrific splash and the engine went dead. Water began to come in under the doors and flow over the floor. We could hear it gurgling outside. Guy got out into the swirling water and waded to the bonnet, but the engine was hopelessly wet. We decided to push the car through the deepest part until the exhaust pipe was clear. So we pushed with all our might and finally achieved this, but it was still impossible to start the engine. We spent a cold, supperless, and cramped night in the car, with mud covering the floor. At dawn

Ants mating in air

Grey-backed shrike

Baby mantises with egg case

Old wagon wheel

Murray woke feeling sick. He was sick twice: then developed diarrhoea to add to his own and the general discomfort. Chirpie began to tell us that she was hungry. The insects we had caught at the school were long since finished so I hunted for more in the thigh-high, soaking grasses of the roadside. Much later, when the river had gone down, an Anti-Stock-Theft Unit land rover came by and stopped to try to help us get the car going – but it was no use. They kindly telephoned from a police post for a vehicle to tow us to Nanyuki. By the time the car was fixed and we got home over roads still running with water, it was four o'clock in the afternoon. The only one of us still cheerful was Chirpie.

Chirpie now lived completely free, leaving or entering her room where she slept perched on the central lamp-shade, by way of a missing window-pane. She came to us whenever she saw us in the garden, and sometimes we took her out in the car to visit ranch projects, having to stop now and again for insect hunts to keep pace with her phenomenal appetite. Other Speke's weavers were building nests at this time and one little male, watching Chirpie feeding on my hand, tried to join her there; but although his feet sometimes actually touched my hand, he never quite dared to settle because each time he came down, Chirpie got a fright and flew off explosively.

Chirpie would nibble our fingers, faces and hair affectionately when we talked to her. She would join us suddenly at meals; and when, for a few days I was unwell in bed with a heavy cold and temperature, caused by our night in the car, she visited me regularly, appearing at my door or window with loud and cheerful cheeps before flying straight for my face. As Bhageera the black cat was always on my bed, I had to throw the covers over him when Chirpie came in, then take her quickly to her room for a token feed of crumbs. But by now she was more or less self supporting, and one day she disappeared. On the third day after this I got up early to search for her and hearing answers to my calls, followed the sound beyond the stables, where Chirpie flew to my hand. Next day she was in the top of the river paddock with a flock of female weavers, and would not come to me. We thought we might not see her again, but that evening I heard her in the garden. She came at once and put her beak between my lips as if asking for food. She took some wholemeal bread, after which she flew to a Pepper tree over the children's room, and after some hesitation went into one of the unoccupied weaver's nests there. We could see her moving about inside it through the unfinished woven bottom, and once she peeped at us through the entrance before settling there for the night. From then on she stayed with the wild weavers. Occasionally we heard her unmistakable chirp, but gradually this baby-call was given up. Chirpie had flown for good.

ELEPHANTS

I had dreamed, that
Sometime in the future I had lived,
And wished to see the mammals of the Miocene.
And it was granted! Huge chocolate hides
Looming in the green I have seen,
And heard the portent of their voices in the gloom.
Round-headed bulls, their pondering bulk,
And angular cows; bearing before them on their brows
Great white teeth.

I have seen the serpentining
Trunks ands fanning, monstrous ears;
Mighty-pillared legs like moving trees
Pushing through the squamous ways their knees,
Treading a path from dinosaur to now;
And in that edificial bulk, that doughty hulk,
Grace and power combined.
But where, tomorrow, I had been,
Elephants weren't found.

Past, Future and a White Rainbow

When Guy came to El Karama he had already become a professional hunter. He continued this career doing nearly all his hunting with clients on his own land. So the wild life, while increasing steadily, contributed significantly to the income of the ranch. A very few times I accompanied Guy when he hunted for meat, and I remember the first occasion. We had been walking for a while when we caught sight of an impala ram ahead, standing looking at us. In the same instant Guy sat down, there was a loud bang and the impala was dead! It was all over, from the sighting of the impala to it's death, in the time it took for one of my feet to pass the other. I was astonished, for normally Guy is a thoughtful, slow and deliberate person. But when he sees the right opportunity during a hunt he acts upon it with extraordinary speed, although preparation for that moment may take hours.

Pleasure in a legitimate hunt for food, one carried out on foot, with skill and careful selection, as it is done here, is different of course from the hideous perversion of enjoying taking life and destroying beauty, or the unsportsmanlike procedure of hunting from a vehicle. But unless a hunter is compassionate and responsible towards his quarry his hunting is contemptible. Sometimes I found looking after hunting clients in our home difficult, and later, Guy would not have wanted to take up professional hunting again, though it provided a third of our income. His difficulties were of a different kind to mine. When setting out one day to look for game-birds, Guy was astonished when a gun went off without warning almost in his ear. His Italian client had blasted off at a Superb starling, the first bird he had seen upon leaving the house. After that, clients did not carry their own firearm until the legitimate quarry had been sighted and was within range.

But sport hunting once meant that all the wild country in Kenya that was not National Park, privately owned, or tribal reserve, was divided into hunting blocks with their own, at that time usually very dedicated, game wardens. This meant less poaching and much more wild life. Country to the North that used to be full of wild life (including rhinos) during the hunting era when I first came to the

458 Winchester Magnum (model 70 super grade)

country, is almost empty of it now; and the rhinos disappeared immediately after the hunting ban of 1977. Recently other factors have come into play to reduce wild life still farther, such as increased human population and domestic animals, and the proliferation of automatic weapons.

When hunting was banned in Kenya, we put up a camp for visitors by the river, using tents that had been the equipment of hunting safaris. When these began to rot they were replaced by thatched, one roomed houses (bandas). There are other places along the river, shaded by Yellow-thorns, which are let to companies who bring tourists to camp. But these activities make little income yet compared to the old hunting.

Animals with snares biting deeply into their necks or legs are frequently seen nowadays, and usually have to be shot. We have had to instigate special snare-patrols. For twenty years the giraffe populations of the ranch averaged four hundred, but recently has suddenly decreased drastically to well below one hundred and continues to decline. It is said that whistling thorn, when heavily browsed over a number of years, develops concentrations of tannins which can poison browsers. Perhaps this has played an important part in moving giraffes away from El Karama, but it is not the full story, for they have decreased elsewhere too. Lines of snares have been found along the river and in bushy places, and great cables are set up high to catch giraffes. Sometimes our cattle are also caught in snares. Hunting parties with packs of dogs have brought waterbuck and oryx to bay, speared them, and cutting up the meat with the speed of practice have disappeared before the place could be reached, even if we set out immediately after the dogs were first heard. Poisoned arrows are also used.

Hope for the future of the wild animals lies, perhaps, in the recent founding of landowners' associations to try to conserve and use wild life for the benefit of all. Only time will tell if the wild creatures, spirit and incarnation of the land, will survive in Laikipia.

✻

Walking out one afternoon to paint, I noticed a magnificent, darkly-marked bull giraffe standing under an acacia tree. Through binoculars I saw that there was a snare of the strongest gauge of wire twisted round his neck, along one side of his body and around a hind leg. Behind him trailed a springy, looping mass. It would be only a matter of time before that dragging wire caught on something and jerked tighter. But because the wire had not yet cut into the giraffe's neck we thought that it might be possible to remove it. The Kenya Wildlife Service, then newly formed, agreed to send an expert on animal immobilisation, and the next morning he arrived, bringing a learner assistant.

Beisa Oryx

Whistling thorn galls with cocktail ants

Poachers, El Karama
May 1994

We found the bull in a large herd of other giraffes, and manoeuvred the vehicle as near to him as possible without disturbing them. The assistant shot first but the dart jumped out without delivering its full charge. At once the bull made off at a stately, ground-eating walk. We followed for almost a mile before there was a chance to fire another dart. By then the first was beginning to have some effect but just as the assistant fired again, the giraffe broke into a canter caus-

Poachers sketched from life, running away after they had seen me

ing him to miss. By the time we had retrieved the dart, the bull was some distance away. This time the expert took the dart-gun and putting his foot on the accelerator, tore across country after the giraffe. We caught up just as the bull was crossing the long drift above Murera dam, and Dick made a perfect shot. We waited for the giraffe to go down. He was now drifting eastwards in an unco-ordinated manner towards an area of erosion. I thought that if he went in there he might never get out. Just then he staggered and toppled backwards into a washout gully. With all the safe places to go down in that he could have chosen, he had made a bee-line for the most dangerous!

Dick cut the wire with a pair of giant pliers, took a blood sample from an ear and injected the antidote. It seemed a long time before the drug took effect though it cannot have been more than five minutes. When the bull made his first convulsive effort to get up, he fell head downwards into the bottom of the gully. It was quite impossible for the four of us to move him at all, for he must have weighed well over a ton. So the Land Rover's winch cable was put round his neck and a rope tied to his horns, and the next time he heaved we managed to get his head onto the side of the gully. I had to operate the winch as the men felt I was not strong enough to pull at the tree-like legs and huge head, as they were doing; but I was afraid that the mechanised winch might break the giraffe's neck. At his next heave the bull fell back into the gully. It was no good. The Land Rover was sent to the house to bring poles and more men to try to lever the animal's huge bulk into a position from which he might be able to get his feet under him. It seemed to take forever for the vehicle to return, and by then the giraffe had already been down

He broke into a canter

longer than was safe for him. But the levers, in conjunction with winch and rope, worked. The bull, after some terrifying flails of neck and legs, rose with a final convulsive heave, dwarfing the people around him. He stood quite still, looking down at us; then walked slowly away. We burst into the almost hysterical laughter of relief.

The wild mammals of El Karama outnumber by far the domestic, and there are more than seventy-five different kinds, not including some of the mice, shrews and bats that we have not yet identified, so that the total may exceed eighty species. This includes some twenty-two different kinds of predator; yet, owing to methods of husbandry based on the traditional African pattern of herding and bomas, we have never had very serious problems with any of these. Bird, insect, reptile, amphibian, fish and plant species together are very many, and wonderfully diverse. We pray that El Karama will always be so blessed, and that other places all over the world may be so, as attitudes to the beauty and usefulness of natural diversity become more enlightened.

Our ranch seems to me to be a kind of organism, in which the cattle, wild animals, and approximately forty-one human families live in symbiosis with the land. In the past, everything achieved has been regulated by the ability and potential of the organism itself. There were no large infusions of outside funds or aid, no subsidies, to give a spurious prosperity. It has been nearly always a struggle to pay the bills and wages. Yet it seems to me that to keep a 'small' ranch like El Karama alive and healthy as Guy, with the help of his men, has done all these years, while the natural system in which it has its being remains intact, is a very great achievement. To be such a rancher takes faith, vision and true grit.

Like a living thing, the ranch is never static, and there have always been changes. But with enormously increasing costs it becomes harder for it to remain viable. New ways will have to be found to make it so. It remains to be seen if that can be done in the twenty-first century.

✻

After spending a night with my dog Wasp in a tent above Murera dam, with Laria and her dog Tinka in another tent beside us, we awoke to an orange sky reflected in the dam, which was like a cauldron of molten metal. Gradually it became lighter until it was as light as full day, but the sun was still behind the horizon. A few

Young Aardwolves

Agamid lizard sunning

A bee-hive (Kenya top bar)

Wasp, daughter of Sambu

PAST, FUTURE AND A WHITE RAINBOW

White rainbow

feathery pink and mauve clouds floated over the mountain, which was a grey-blue silhouette. In the hollows and on some of the higher ridges was a white mist and though the trees were beginning to be touched with gold, some were still only grey shadows. Then the sun came up, and it had a gentle warmth to it. We began to walk down the slope of the Bat-eared fox Plain to a big rock, and it seemed to me that never before had I seen such beauty as there was that morning. The grass was so heavily rimed with dew that it appeared the colour of pale jade, and everywhere were little Pentanisia flowers, bluer than the sky. Zebras grazed peacefully, not knowing we were there, and a herd of waterbuck hinds stood to stare. In the mukinyea trees beyond the rock, an eland cow walked past without seeing us. Giraffes came slowly up behind us, inquisitive, and two others were sparring, only their waving heads appearing above a brow of land, mysteriously disembodied. The animals seemed unafraid, and I was quite without my usual worry of meeting buffaloes. It was inconceivable there could be danger on such a morning. The air was full of mist droplets like microscopic pearls, that rose and fell in front of my eyes with each step I took, and felt damp and cool on my skin. New zebra foals must see these water-droplets and wonder at them, as they must wonder at everything in such a world. As Wasp and I came out of the gully and up the other side onto the flanks of Giraffe Ridge, the sun shining from behind on the mist ahead made a white rainbow. I have never seen such a thing before or since. It was a thickening of the vapour in a perfect bow over the way we were walking. This bow lasted a long time, and was still there when we were nearly back at our camp. Then, the ordinary light of day commenced; the ethereal, ephemeral magic of dawn disappeared, and with it the white rainbow – though there was still a little mist in the valleys.

Termite hill, January 2000